FAITH, HOPE, ACTION

USHERING IN A NEW EARTH ERA, TOGETHER

DIANA J. ENSIGN, J.D.

Book cover by Arcane Book Cover Designs. Quotes from the book, *Dirt to Soil*, were used with permission of the author.

Published by SpiritHawk Life Publications
Indianapolis, Indiana USA

Library of Congress Control Number 2024902740.
Ensign, Diana
Title: Faith, Hope, Action: ushering in a new earth era, together/ Diana J. Ensign—1st edition p. cm.

ISBN: 978-0-9883320-3-4 (paperback)
ISBN: 978-0-9883320-4-1(ebook)

Subjects: 1. Nature Writing – Nature conservation – Religious aspects – Christianity 2. Environmental protection

PRAISE FOR DIANA ENSIGN'S
FAITH, HOPE, ACTION

"Tackling the climate change crisis is a task so overwhelming that it stops most people from doing anything. Diana Ensign (who won WATER's Rosemary Ganley Essay Contest) breaks it down into doable chunks, offering something for everyone to try. *Faith, Hope, Action,* with its concrete examples, helps and challenges us. Whether building a house with recycled materials, probing one's faith tradition for inspiration, or eating healthily grown food, the options are endless: And the need is now!"
—Mary E. Hunt, PhD, Co-Director, Women's Alliance for Theology, Ethics, and Ritual (WATER)

"Diana Ensign's *Faith, Hope, Action* connects the reader to current environmental challenges that may seem overwhelming at first, but she provides timely wisdom and guidance on ways everyone can take meaningful action to help our Earth."
—Ellen Jacquart, Program Leader for Indiana Native Plant Society and former ecologist at The Nature Conservancy

"In *Faith, Hope, Action,* Diana Ensign brings her passion for practical spirituality to the essential subject of Earth care. Her pragmatic insights remind us that we are the eyes, feet, and hands of God's presence. We open our minds to the Divine Mind, download Divine Ideas that are appropriate for each of us, and engage our passions to make this world a better place. We'll do amazing things together.

Despair is not an option! We know what to do, and we do it."

—Reverend Bob Uhlar, MS, Unity Minister, former Broadcast Journalist (WMAQ-AM; WBBM-AM Chicago), Kerrville, TX

"*Faith, Hope, Action* is a poetic pilgrimage in which Diana Ensign follows the longing of heart, body, and spirit to live in reverent communion with living Earth. She bravely adds her voice to the growing global chorus of people who dare to speak out against our society's addicted, Earth-destroying systems. We must return home, she urges, by healing, learning, and daring to change. As Diana invites us into her own life-changing journey, we find the courage to come home to Earth renewed."

—Liza Hyatt, Poet, Art Therapist, author of *Art of the Earth: Ancient Art for a Green Future*, and Founder of Earth Monk monastic community

"In this captivating book, *Faith, Hope, Action*, Diana Ensign emphasizes the profound connection between nurturing our well-being and restoring harmony to our planet. By embracing a lifestyle that prioritizes our health, we not only heal our bodies but also contribute to the healing of our precious Earth. The act of consuming nourishing, wholesome food becomes a powerful tool, enabling us to care for ourselves, our loved ones, and our shared home on this magnificent planet."

—Carole Bishop, Co-Owner Pure Eating Way LLC, www.pureeatingway.com

"With deep love for nature and our children, *Faith, Hope, Action* highlights the critical need for our communities to adopt renewable energy and to advocate for green initiatives that make our world a better place."
—Leslie Webb, Co-Founder and President Carmel Green Initiative, https://www.carmel green.org/

"*Faith, Hope, Action* is a welcome reflection on the need for urgency in caring for our planet and our fellow global inhabitants. Climate change and environmental destruction have pushed us to the brink of global resilience while we assume the planet will keep providing resources without constraints and without regard to the critical stabilizing role that nature provides. Diana Ensign's urgent message is that we need to care for our earth and care for one another. Woven into this very personal narrative is a love of nature, a practice of deep listening, and a concern for future generations. Most importantly, this book imparts the message that change occurs in community and in conversation with each other."
—Gabriel Filippelli, PhD, Executive Director, Indiana University Environmental Resilience Institute, and author of *Climate Change and Life*.

"Diana Ensign's *Faith, Hope, Action* is packed full of environmental and climate issues that are being observed by everyday people, such as the decline of lightening bugs that were once abundant on summer nights. A change from industrial farming dependent on chemicals to regenerative farming practices improves the ecological system by producing healthier produce and a biodiverse habitat. Her book highlights the impact of human activities on our environment and the social injustice of industrial pollution on minority communities. Our elected officials need to address these concerns by encouraging the use of renewable energy and by cleaning up hazardous chemicals. The strength of Faith, Hope, Action is an offering of common-sense solutions that have been proven to work."

—Ron Rhoads, Climate Reality Leader, Heartland Chapter

"Diana Ensign's thoughtful, in-depth, and insightful book, *Faith, Hope, Action*, illuminates a path for all to follow. Her passion to heal encourages everyone, each in their own unique way, to be part of the solution for the most challenging issues of our time. Diana's inspiring message brings to mind a quote from Cesar Chavez, 'It starts with your heart and radiates out.'"

—Charlie Wiles, Executive Director, Center for Interfaith Cooperation

Faith, Hope, Action is beautifully written with so much wisdom. I love Diana Ensign's words: all of them. A respectful and sweeping perspective that gives hope, vision, and practical ideas for folks who care about our beautiful planet: a balm for the anxiety and grief so many of us feel! A highly recommended read for both a present and future people on a planet whose life-support system is in trouble. So grateful that this book allows our energy to turn to useful, helpful actions.

—Dr. Candace Corson, MD, CEO of Corson Wellness, LLC

"From my Christian faith perspective, all humanity has the responsibility for ensuring we live respectfully of the abundance entrusted to us by our Creator for the good of all. Diana Ensign's book, *Faith, Hope, Action*, beautifully illus-

trates the intricacy of human relationships to their ecosystems. She has shown how positive, Earth-conscious actions result in life-affirming change for the whole Earth."
—Reverend Amber Good, Faith & Ecology Education Director Teter Retreat & Organic Farm, Noblesville First United Methodist Church

"Diana Ensign invites us to join her on her journey to reconnect with nature and offers reflections on the importance of both personal and collaborative action in protecting our common home, Earth. She sketches the many environmental challenges we face, including the existential threat of climate change, and quickly pivots to solutions. Diana's thoughtful and encouraging approach is well-suited to inspiring action for anyone who has ever felt overwhelmed by dire reports of climate change."
—Lani Ethridge, Citizens' Climate Lobby, Evansville Chapter

"Diana Ensign's *Faith, Hope, Action* is a wonderful distillation of how climate justice is inextricably linked to all other forms of justice. The injustices our society perpetuates that most heavily impact poor, migrant, and BIPOC (Black, Indigenous, People of Color) communities —among other marginalized beloveds—are often directly related to our lack of careful stewardship for our shared world. *Faith, Hope, Action* provides a life-giving perspective for the care of all we love, and I am grateful that we are finally saying so out loud!"
—Reverend Misha Sanders, Northwest Unitarian Universalist Congregation, GA

"In order to change an existing paradigm, you do not struggle to try and change the problematic model. You create a new model and make the old one obsolete."

— R. BUCKMINSTER FULLER, INVENTOR,
ENVIRONMENTAL ACTIVIST

TABLE OF CONTENTS

PREFACE

"One should pay attention to even the smallest crawling creature for these too may have a valuable lesson to teach us."

— BLACK ELK, OGLALA LAKOTA (SIOUX)
MEDICINE MAN

On a visit to the sprawling farmlands in Southern Indiana, I met with Dorothy, who is ninety-one years old. She was telling me that she saw more fireflies in her yard this past summer than she has seen since she was a girl. She said, "I haven't seen that many fireflies in over sixty-five years! It was amazing!"

The landscape near Dorothy's home—where she and her husband have lived for close to seventy years and where they raised their seven children—has undergone drastic (some would say radical) changes of late. An abutting 300-acre corn and soybean farm owned by her brother is now being managed by his son, Pat. Pat is a firm believer in regenerative farming. Just a few years ago, he began planting diverse native wildflowers as cover crops and stopped tilling the soil. Under Pat's management, the family farm also significantly decreased its use of pesticides and chemical fertilizers. As Pat explained to me:

"The companies developing and selling deadly chemicals during World War II needed a new market for their products when the war ended. That's how we came to have all these harmful poisons being used on our farmlands and on our crop seeds, which are also coated with toxic pesticides. Farmers till the land—killing the earthworms and plant roots—and then add chemicals to eliminate insects and bacteria, and we end up with dead soil."

He notes that studies have shown substantial nutritional decline (lower levels of vitamins and minerals) in our fruits and vegetables because of farm soil depletion. The result of Pat's regenerative farming efforts is healthier soil that results in better nutrition in the food crops.

An added bonus: Pat has witnessed a return of wildlife! The soil now contains worms, and the diverse native cover crops bring needed insects like bees, butterflies, and other pollinators, along with a multitude of songbirds. Eagles and hawks soar over his land, and quail make their home in a woodpile at the edge of the property. This healthy soil with deep roots from native plants also absorbs rainfall better, acting as a sponge to help alleviate flooding. What is more, the water on his land no longer contains all the harsh chemical poisons that run off into neighboring streams and water supplies. Finally, these healthier land practices store carbon dioxide in the soil, a critical step in combatting global warming.

Just this one person doing his small bit of good on this piece of land has benefited the entire ecosystem, including the arrival of lightning bugs in Dorothy's adjoining yard.

Anyone who has watched Ken Burns's documentary, *The Dust Bowl*, understands that what we do to the land can either carry enormous gifts—nutritious food, abundant wildlife, and clean water—or cause escalating devastation. The choice is ours to make. A well-known quote from Indigenous teachings reminds us, "What we do to the Earth, we do to ourselves."

I am sharing Pat's story because we each have tremendous power to make a positive difference in our local and global communities. We know destructive practices are still taking place across the planet, causing increased flooding, fires, droughts, air pollution, unsafe drinking water, diseases, warming temperatures, climate disruptions, and species extinction. We, likewise, know climate change is here and that we are responsible for our part in causing damage to our Earth home.

According to NASA and as cited by Anthony Leiserowitz, PhD, a research scientist at Yale, "97% of climate scientists have concluded that human-caused global warming is happening." Leiserowitz sums it up as follows: "Scientists agree: It's real. It's happening. It's bad. . . . But there is hope."

Fortunately, there are *numerous* actions we can take to help heal our planet, actions that lead us forward in nourishing ways. It's merely a matter of implementing Earth-friendly practices and adopting healthier behaviors in harmony with Mother Earth.

Although Pat's regenerative farming practices are a wonderful illustration of one individual making beneficial changes in his local community, it's going to take ALL OF US working together to solve our global environmental challenges. Consider, for example, the widely reported story of the children who got trapped inside a flooded cave in Thailand. No one person had the solution for how to get them out safely, and no one person rescued them. It was the cooperative teamwork of countless people from across the globe working in unison with lots of ideas and a shared goal: to help save children caught in a dire, life-threatening situation.

Saving our Earth home for all children requires the same dedication, teamwork, urgency, and creative problem-solving. It requires us to work together for the common welfare of everyone.

With each healthy seed we plant, literally and metaphorically, we will cultivate seeds of wellness. Our actions then nourish collective seeds of change, seeds of courage, seeds of compassion, seeds of hope, and seeds of love. Ultimately, our combined daily choices will create our wholesome earthly gardens. But we no longer have the luxury of time to argue and fight. We must begin implementing as many solutions as possible. As the saying goes, "If you are not part of the solution, then you are part of the problem."

So let us begin, this day, working for future generations of children who will look back at our commitments, our values, and our actions and say:

"Thank you for showing us how to take care of our Earth home, and thank you for protecting the land, creatures, water, and air so that we have healthy food, healthy bodies, healthy minds, and joyful spirits."

INTRODUCTION

WHERE DO WE START?

When I was in elementary school, I'd race outside during recess with my best friend, Germaine, as we headed for an enormous field behind the playground area. We'd pretend we were wild horses galloping through the tall grass. At that age, our imaginations were limitless and took us on incredible adventures. Later, when I had children of my own, I watched them playing with neighborhood friends in a backyard bursting with wild violets, white clover, and yellow dandelions; rambling up the wide branches of their favorite climbing tree in a nearby park; or collecting brightly colored stones from Lake Huron's rocky shoreline during summer vacations.

Do you still remember the childhood pleasures of simply being outdoors: marveling at the sky, the trees, and the ground beneath your feet? Remember late at night listening to crickets? Or watching a fuzzy caterpillar slowly inch its ways across the sidewalk? Or perhaps gazing in wonder at the long, sleek body of a lone praying mantis?

Sadly, with our penchant for spraying pesticides and destroying habitat, some of these tiny creatures may be harder to find now.

Somewhere along the way, humans seem to have forgotten how to appreciate nature's abundant gifts. Maybe we got too busy with work and no longer had time to pay attention to sunlight filtering through the tree tops, or to watch a hawk soaring high above in a vivid blue sky, or to observe an otter swimming along the river's edge. Maybe some of us grew up in congested cities and in less-than-idyllic environments devoid of nature's wonders. Of course, children and adults across the world today are scavenging for food, drinking unsafe water, and working in toxic environments to make products purchased by the wealthy. While I love the beauty of this magnificent planet, I don't want any of us to ignore the hardships faced by people who are living in impoverished, unhealthy conditions.

My own escape—from the violence I witnessed in my childhood home—was through stories I began writing at age twelve. Growing up, I watched the adults in my household working long hours, fighting over finances, and my stepfather drinking to excess. Imaginative play and outdoor explorations were gone by the time I entered middle school. "Time to leave the enchanted forest," as Owl might say to Christopher Robin in a *Winnie-the-Pooh* storybook.

In school, we filled our brains with the names of presidents, the state capitals, the Pledge of Allegiance to the flag, and the conquests of territories and of people. I was not taught how to care for our Earth or how to practice good stewardship toward the land upon which we depend for our survival. I did not learn about the genocide of Native Americans in the United States nor the displacement and killings of Indigenous Peoples across the globe. I did not learn about racial inequality. I did not learn about the horrific pollution from the Industrial Revolution and the harms of global warming from the burning of fossil fuels. I did not learn about the deadly air pollution from the burning of coal, the poisonous chemicals from plastics, and the cruelty of animal factory farms. Just to be clear, people *knew* about these ills and systemic injustices back in my childhood. Governments, scientists, and businesses have known of these atrocities for a very long time. (More about that in upcoming chapters.) Yet, such truths did not get passed along in my educational curriculum. Or worse, alarming facts were intentionally covered up by the people profiting from damaging practices and oppressive systems.

Despite this deliberate and ongoing lack of transparency regarding such wrongs, more of us now understand that all of these issues are interconnected. How we care for one another and how we care for our Earth home affects *everything*.

Current-day school curriculums, hopefully, include accurate portrayals of history and scientific Earth-care knowledge that I failed to receive growing up. If so, are government representatives and business leaders paying attention and setting good examples for our youth? Or are they ignoring what the students and their teachers have to say about environmental justice and about the sustainable, eco-friendly changes desperately needed for our planet's survival—and our own?

For adults not raised with the awareness of these destructive actions, how do we unlearn all the years of conditioning that have put systems of profit above the health and safety of humanity? How do we step aside for a moment, pause, and acknowledge that we need to learn new ways?

A YEARLONG EARTH QUEST

Anyone familiar with twelve-step programs knows that denial is a hindrance to constructive change. Admitting difficult truths is often an essential first step on the path to recovery. Likewise with our environmental devastation, we have to admit that WE have a serious problem, and WE ARE THE PROBLEM, in order to do the necessary work needed for healthy living. Our present mode of doing business and governing our lives on Mother Earth has become unmanageable.

Toward that end, I resolved to spend a year exploring the following questions:

- *What harmful human actions are causing our environmental crisis?*
- *How do we learn to work together to solve the challenges we face?*
- *What positive actions can we take to benefit our Earth home and all of Earth's inhabitants?*

That is how my Earth chronicles began, with a yearlong commitment to delving into these urgent questions regarding the care of our shared home. While I recognize that one book cannot possibly address every environmental problem—or every potential solution in this rapidly changing landscape of research and innovation—I remind myself that we will never get anything done if we wait for the perfect time or the perfect answer before we begin to act.

Consequently, despite feeling overwhelmed by the enormity of the challenges we face, I devoted a year to meeting with environmental leaders—including environmental justice advocates—and attending educational forums on an array of ecological topics. In the process, I learned about faith-based Earth stewardship measures. I visited regenerative farming communities. I listened to Indigenous teachers with a long tradition of honoring our sacred Earth, and I sat down with student activists to hear their perspective on caring for our Earth home.

One of my strengths is my ability to listen, a skill I utilize in each writing project. I don't know if I came into this world as a quiet observer or if it is a trauma-based survival mechanism I developed growing up. In either case, I listened attentively to numerous knowledgeable people throughout the course of this project. I also read environmental books, science-based articles, and reports by nonprofit organizations. Moreover, I spent ample time in nature to connect with Mother Earth, listening to the birds, the rain, the trees, and the wind. Nature has much to teach us as well.

Like any big undertaking, my one-year project soon turned into two years, with learning that will, no doubt, continue throughout my life. Along the way, I discovered that asking and answering questions about how to care for our Earth does not result in one magic solution. Instead, it is an evolving process that spirals upward, toward positive growth, as we learn more about what is needed and make the healthy changes required of us.

How do we do so?

We begin by healing ourselves, healing our communities, and healing our Earth. By remaining open to diverse sources of wisdom. By living in balance and in harmony with Mother Earth. And by remembering to act from a place of deep reverence and love—for ourselves, for each other, and for our shared Earth home.

WHY THIS BOOK?

I am a mother and may someday have grandchildren. I want all the Earth's children to be able to play outdoors and grow up healthy and happy. I want us to live in a world that is peaceful, with people who are working each day toward making our planet a nourishing place to live. In short, I am writing this book because I care. Of course, it certainly doesn't require having children to care. I know lots of people who are not parents, and yet they most definitely worry about the well-being of future generations and work passionately to protect our Earth.

I also enjoy spending time outdoors watching birds, hiking, swimming, and exploring. I love trees! I love sunrises, lakes, oceans, rivers, forests, mountains, sunsets, deer, foxes, dolphins, and whales. I love fresh blueberries, ripe peaches, and juicy strawberries. I love summer sunshine, fall foliage, winter walks, and spring flowers. I love Earth! In fact, it's not just that I enjoy the outdoors, I *need* time in nature to recharge my spirit. When I walk outside in nature's abundant beauty, even if it's just a brief visit to a local park, I feel happy. My deep spiritual connection is with the natural world. I find solace among the trees and inner peace while watching the early morning sunrise. For me, nature is both restorative and profoundly healing.

Finally, I am a writer. It is who I am. Writing has not necessarily been an easy path. But it is, I believe, my soul's purpose. It is what I do in this world whenever something tugs at my heart. As such, this book is a spiritual endeavor as a human living on this planet, and it is not meant to be an academic or scientific treatise—though I do try to credit the scientists and academics who lent their vast expertise to this critical topic. When I spend years of my life working on a book, it is my goal for the writing to be of service.

This journey, which started as a desire to use my skills to make a meaningful difference, has resulted in the Earth-care chronicles I now share with you. I am writing this particular book because if the planet dies, everything we love will be gone, and all the things we waste time fighting about won't matter. I want to do my part to help.

Perhaps that is what is being asked from each of us: to take some small action and not wait any longer for someone else to solve our problems. Joining together in these efforts, we can then create a new paradigm that entails healthier ways of being in the world and with each other as we work to safeguard our Earth home.

WEAVING A NEW EARTH STORY

Taking a few slow breaths, I gaze over at the purple-pink coneflowers in my backyard. It's early autumn in my part of the world, the Midwestern United States, and a few flowers still have their petals. I see a spider and her web near the dried echinacea seedheads; a few strands of the finely woven web catch the afternoon light. A web is a symbol: all things are intricately connected. The spider is the weaver. She is the creator and a representation of the Divine Feminine.

So, I ask: What new Earth story will we weave? What web will we craft with our thoughts, our words, and our deeds? How will we mend the web when fragile strands have been torn?

I recall a quote from the Talmud: *"Do not be daunted by the enormity of the world's grief. Do justly, now. Love mercy, now. Walk humbly, now. . . . You are not obligated to complete the work, but neither are you free to abandon it."*

I watch as a hummingbird hovers briefly over a patch of bee balm flowers in search of nectar, carrying an encouraging message of hope on her swiftly fluttering wings:

"It's not too late to care."

PART ONE
FAITH

CHAPTER ONE
INTO THE WOODS

"We are not called upon to do all the good that is possible, but only that which we can do."

— SAINT MOTHER THEODORE GUERIN

A WINTER RETREAT

After a few months of planning, today I arrive at Saint Mary-of-the-Woods to stay at a retreat hermitage nestled near a quiet, wooded terrain in Northwest Indiana. My hermitage is a small, eco-friendly house with one bedroom and a combined kitchen/living area. A back deck looks out onto a frozen lake as well as the woods beyond. I'm drinking a cup of hot tea and feeling grateful to be here. The glass doors leading to the deck allow for a splendid view of nature from the couch. It's late in the day, so I'll wait until tomorrow to explore. I'm hoping the sunrise will be visible from the deck as it's situated toward the east.

I notice a nuthatch hopping up a nearby tree trunk and observe an abundance of crumpled, brown leaves covering the hard, cold ground, likely providing the tiny creatures living below with an insulated, warm abode. Earlier, as I was driving along the dirt road—the last turnoff before arriving at my hermitage—a large hawk had greeted me from a lone tree near a bend in the road. Although not a birch tree, all the branches were white. Maybe a result of the tree bark that peeled off after a winter frost? The regal red-tailed hawk, perched stately upon one of these branches with its chest puffed slightly out, acted as though he or she had been appointed the overseer of the surrounding territory. I took the hawk's presence as a good omen while embarking on this solitary excursion to connect with the deeper self, the land, the water, the air, and the wildlife. I have no immediate plans or agenda beyond this simple beginning—to spend quiet time at Saint Mary-of-the-Woods in a hermitage beside the lake.

I chose this retreat location because of the White Violet Center for Eco-Justice, a ministry of the Sisters of Providence focused on organic agriculture, spiritual ecology, and social advocacy. Passionate about the conservation of our sacred Earth, the Sisters of Providence tend to the orchards, bee hives, a five-acre organic garden, a farm store, various farm animals, and a nature trail here at Saint Mary-of-the-Woods (nicknamed "the Woods").

Outside near the back deck, I see a gray squirrel sitting upright in the crook of a tree while gnawing away on a nut. Its tail is extended up over its back like a fluffy scarf while its paws tightly clench this evening's dinner. The squirrel has a pleasant view of the lake as well.

Stepping outdoors for a moment, I see a swirled configuration in the center of the lake's frozen surface. I wonder what could have caused those circles. Water currents? Wind? Something dumped below that leaked out and bubbled up to the surface? Near the lake's edge, a large tree—having floated to its current spot—is firmly lodged in the frozen waters. It has dried purplish leaves still attached to the outstretched limbs while the trunk remains buried beneath the ice. What tree has small purplish leaves? Japanese maple? Crabapple?

My preference for a retreat would have been in spring or summer when the air is warm and the flowers and plants are in full bloom. Yet, perhaps the quiet slumber of winter will serve me well for going within and listening. Like the stillness of the tree submerged in the frozen lake, I will take some time to discover what lies hidden far below the surface.

Back indoors, I unpack. I brought some homemade soup with me. It has an abundance of organic carrots, lentils, yams, ginger, and chopped celery. I also brought Fair Trade organic coffee, chamomile lavender tea, organic oats, and some dried cranberries. I have already decided no social media or television while I'm here. In quietude, I can commune more closely with nature and with my own inner reflections. If I close my eyes, I can imagine myself as a giant bear, snug and cozy within the warmth of my den.

I packed a couple of nature book classics for reading material: *Silent Spring* by Rachel Carson and *A Sand County Almanac* by Aldo Leopold. I also brought *Blue Covenant* by Maude Barlow, *Saving Us* by Katharine Hayhoe, and *No One Is Too Small to Make a Difference*, a collection of Greta Thunberg's speeches. Before beginning this retreat, I had some trepidation about how to fill my time alone in the midst of winter without the usual distractions of daily to-do lists and evening television shows. I am happy to report that I've found a soft blue blanket to curl up in and within just a few short hours of my arrival, I am at peace with my decision.

A pair of cardinals suddenly alight on a low tree limb

near the deck. The bright red male cardinal stands out
starkly against the drab winter landscape. The grayish
female, with only a hint of red on her wings and head, is
much more subtle in appearance than her male counter-
part. I have heard that the vibrant colors of the male birds
serve a courting and mating purpose. Could it also be that
their bright colors are a distraction to keep the female
safe? I'm not a biologist, but as a woman here on my own,
safety is a consideration, especially as I have set up my
retreat pilgrimage in an unfamiliar place.

I wonder if being less visible in the world *really* protects
us? Perhaps if women had held *more* influential positions
throughout history, they would have prevented the (cen-
turies-old) violence perpetuated by men against women.
It's hard to imagine all the ways our lives, and our world,
would be different if patriarchy had not become the domi-
nant ruling order. I wonder how our views of Mother
Earth might have advanced—along with our ideas of
God, religion, art, history, science, philosophy, literature,
music, law, education, medicine, and government—if
women had been in charge?

Finding myself on this land managed by nuns who
have an interest in eco-justice, I believe it's time—past
time—to listen to what women have to say and to try
creating something new. We need a life-sustaining reverence toward our Earth Mother—the vibrant, living organism, providing our first breath of air, our abundant food
sources, and our lifelong home.

As the sun begins its gradual descent in the west, I
hear a far-off train whistle and what sounds like the faint
call of sandhill cranes. One of the most exhilarating sightings and distinct sounds is that of sandhill cranes as they
pass by overhead. I've seen them high in the sky when out
walking through my neighborhood. They are a wonderful
sight to behold.

Glancing outside, I see the sun's fading glow cast a beautiful golden light against the tree trunks. Then, the bright orb of sunlight disappears beyond a low hill that makes up the farmland to the west of the woods. I watch it descend from the bedroom window. I am going to put on my pajamas, curl up in bed, and start perusing my books. I am warm. I am nourished. I will be okay, here on my own, at Saint Mary-of-the-Woods.

Tomorrow, I explore.

THE CAWING OF CROWS

I woke to the cackling sound of crows early this morning. I slept fitfully, hardly getting any rest at all. Being a woman alone, near the woods, can be both a respite and slightly terrifying. Unfortunately, I am more frightened than I care to admit.

I have experienced two incidents where I was out walking in secluded natural areas and found myself in situations where men intended me harm. The first encounter took place decades ago in a wooded area near a college campus. Luckily, when the young men approached me, I was able to make a quick exit onto a nearby trail. The more recent second encounter was not a concern about rape but rather about staying alive. I was on an out-of-town trip—walking up a remote hill-side near the river—when two large gruff-looking men, both wearing overalls, came directly toward me, from different directions, at a rapid pace. I stood upright, straightening my shoulders back, while striding purpose-fully toward the parking lot, and I made a point to visibly dig into my purse as though grabbing something. Seeing my movement, the men simultaneously turned away and bolted back toward the directions they had come from. The fact that I am alive today is astounding

because that situation could easily have had a tragic end
—and for many women, such encounters have resulted
in the loss of life.

I give you these background stories to explain that I
could not sleep because I was afraid—even though my
retreat is in a peaceful setting, even though it is a place run
by nuns, and even though I am perfectly safe. Nonetheless,
the fears that grip the heart aren't always rational and do
often have their roots in both the ancestral and the
modern experience of being a woman in a violent, patri-
archal world where women are not always safe. I also
share these experiences because I believe that how aggres-
sive male predators in our culture treat women is similar
to how some men treat Mother Earth: as an object to
abuse.

Our Earth is a beautiful living organism, teeming with
life. This amazing planet—with flowing waters, towering
trees with intricately connected root systems, and over
140,000 known species of fungi—is very much *alive*. We
are simply one life form on this vast Earth, along with all
the other creatures sustained by air, water, sunlight, and
food.

Is it possible that Mother Earth also feels stress from
historic as well as present-day traumas? Surely humans are
not the only ones to experience distress from ongoing
threatening situations? Aren't scientists learning that tree
root systems and foraging insects have methods for
communicating danger? We know wildlife and marine life
communicate threats to one another in a variety of ways.
Just because most humans no longer hear or feel what
Mother Earth communicates—or what other living beings
transmit—it does not mean stress signals aren't happening.
Ask the scientists, poets, philosophers, and wise sages—
they will tell you. Ask the elders from Indigenous cultures
what they know of Earth's abilities to impart information.

Indigenous Peoples have long listened to Mother Earth to gain insights and wisdom.

I will share one quick story. When my biological father died, I was sitting outside in my yard, lost in grief. After I had finished eating breakfast, I set my bowl of oatmeal down beside me. A squirrel looked up at me from across the driveway. Without thinking, I silently said to the squirrel, *"You can have it,"* and went back to my internal musings about my father's death. The squirrel came over next to me and ate from the bowl. This story is just one example, *of many*, where I know from personal experience that there are ways of communicating and being in this world that are drastically different from our day-to-day consciousness. Most of us aren't raised with that awareness, nor do we have daily mindfulness practices that encourage it. Even so, mystics, monks, Indigenous Peoples, shamans, artists, and intuitive healers from throughout the ages and across the planet understand that our ways of listening, our energetic vibrations, and our ways of being are deeply connected to Mother Earth—known in some cultures as Grandmother Earth, Gaia, Pachamama, and Cosmic Mother.

Regardless of our beliefs about our Earth as a living, interconnected organism that responds to stress, we know that humans transmit anxiety, which can result in second-hand stress for the observer. If you spend much time around someone who is highly anxious or angry, you will no doubt agree. Similarly, humans have the capacity to convey compassion, peace, and love for the benefit of others—which, as the Dalai Lama reminds us, is not a luxury but is "essential to our existence." Dr. Deepak Chopra has conducted studies regarding chemically measurable responses of people in meditation groups, and Dr. Masaru Emoto reported how water molecules respond to sound vibrations. Notably, about 60 percent of the human body is made up of water. Thus, if we choose to do so, we can impart loving-kindness and tenderness toward our Mother Earth—and acknowledge the suffering we've inflicted.

So, I ask again: Is it possible for Mother Earth to experience trauma from ongoing abuses, such as hazardous waste dumps, strip mining, toxic poisons, and clear-cutting of forests?

To answer that question, spend quiet, meditative time in nature and ask Mother Earth yourself . . . and then listen.

You will hear in your heart the answer to your question. You will *feel* the answer you seek in the very essence of your being.

Maybe the questions we must then ask are: *What will help us live in harmony with our Earth home? What will help us appreciate Mother Earth's bountiful gifts?*

DENYING SERIOUS PROBLEMS

I started reading my nature books last night, which may have added to my nighttime restlessness. There is nothing uplifting about the very real health and environmental hazards of pollution, global warming, climate disruptions, water shortages, and species extinction. We've known for so long about the importance of caring for our Earth, going back tens of thousands of years with Indigenous Peoples' deep reverence for nature. We've also known about the risk to our survival if we do not get our predilection for toxic pollutants and our destructive habits under control.

Rachel Carson, a biologist, wrote about the horrendous harms from the use of chemical pesticides and herbicides and their links to human cancer back in the 1960s. At that time, the pesticide DDT was widely being used.

Due to her book *Silent Spring*—and the public outcry and scientific research that followed—the U.S. Environmental Protection Agency later banned DDT in the United States. Like many people who speak out about our environmental ills, she was initially mocked and scorned by the chemical industry. But as Carson correctly noted, the poisons we put into the air, water, and soil will find their way into our bodies and into the bodies of our children. She stated in her book in 1962:

> No longer are exposures to dangerous chemicals occupational alone; they have entered the environment of everyone—even of children as yet unborn. . . . A quarter century ago, cancer in children was considered a medical rarity. Today, more American school children die of cancer than from any other disease. So serious has this situation become that Boston has established the first hospital in the United States devoted exclusively to the treatment of children with cancer.

At present, there are more than 200 children's cancer hospitals in the United States. We likely all know someone who has been diagnosed with cancer, or who has died from cancer, including young children. Science has since proven that toxic chemicals are found in breast milk and throughout the food chain. While genetic factors and lifestyle choices can certainly lead to cancer, why would we think that the poisons we put in our air, water, soil, and food *would not* have deadly results on our bodies and the bodies of our children?

The people I know who have recently died or been diagnosed with cancer have never been cigarette smokers, did not drink excessive amounts of alcohol, and do not have family predispositions to cancer. Yet people are diagnosed and dying from colon cancer, pancreatic cancer, breast cancer, brain cancer, leukemia, thyroid cancer, lung cancer, and so on; and those cancer diagnoses and deaths —among other serious illnesses—include people who eat healthy foods and exercise.

Harvard School of Public Health says that harmful PFAS (perfluoroalkyl and polyfluoroalkyl substances)— known as "forever chemicals" because they don't break down in the environment or in our bodies—are found in everyday products, including food packaging, clothing, cosmetics, and toilet paper. These toxic PFAS are man-made synthetic chemicals, also found in our rivers and lakes. An environmental advocacy group, Clean Water Action, proclaims, "Every American tested has PFAS in their blood." Studies have linked PFAS to cancers, liver problems, thyroid function, decreased fertility, newborn deaths, and other serious health problems.

Toxic chemicals in plastics and microplastics (extremely small plastic pieces) also make their way into the human body and are linked to severe illnesses, including cancers. The Geneva Environment Network (GEN), a global partnership of more than 100 environmental and sustainable development organizations, highlights the deadly harms to our health from plastics. As GEN points out, "Humans are exposed to a large variety of toxic chemicals and microplastics through inhalation, ingestion, and direct skin contact, all along the plastic life-cycle." Citing the World Wildlife Federation, GEN says, "An average person could be ingesting approximately 5 grams of plastic every week. . . . The toxic chemical additives and pollutants found in plastics threaten human health on a global scale."

Environmental pollutants clearly pose dangers to our health. Another example can be found in the harms from coal-generated energy. Harvard Public Health states, "The more a country relies on coal-fired power plants to generate energy, the greater the lung cancer risk is among its citizens." Coal ash, a toxic waste material, is produced whenever coal is burned at coal-fired power plants. According to the Indiana Environmental Reporter (an independent reporting organization supported by The Media School at Indiana University), coal ash—which contains containments such as mercury and arsenic—"has been found in groundwater at every Indiana facility where coal was burned for electricity" and these harmful chemicals pose risks of "neurological and cardiovascular problems, as well as cancer in the skin, bladder, liver and lungs." (See more in the "Hazards of Fossil Fuels" section.)

Carson noted over half a century ago that if we are poisoning our Earth, that means decades of accumulated poisons are being stored in the cells, tissues, and bones of our bodies and in *every* aspect of the food we consume. If we want our bodies to be healthy, and if we want to find a cure for cancer, we must eliminate environmental toxins and hold responsible the industries contributing to the pollutants that harm our health.

HUMAN-CAUSED CLIMATE CHANGE

We have also known about human-caused climate change for a long time. According to climate scientist Katharine Hayhoe, author of *Saving Us*, scientists have known about human-caused global warming for over a century. Hayhoe says:

> Scientists have known since the 1850s that carbon dioxide traps heat. It's been building up in the atmosphere from all the coal, oil, and gas we've burned since the start of the Industrial Revolution to generate electricity, heat our homes, power our factories, and,

eventually, run our cars, ships, and planes. . . . We are the cause of *all* of the observed warming—and then some.

Per Hayhoe, even the oil and gas industry (acting like the tobacco companies before them), studied and knew of the environmental dangers related to their fossil fuel practices based on their own scientific reports. She further adds that, for decades, the Navy tracked the rising sea levels, NASA reported on the harm from human-caused climate change, and the US president knew of these harmful trends as early as the 1960s.

When the then-US president, Jimmy Carter, installed solar panels on the White House in the 1970s and asked families to turn down their heat and conserve energy, not everyone responded to the urgency in his message, including the Reagan administration, which decided to have the solar panels removed. An article in *Scientific American*, a renowned magazine exploring science, knowledge, and technology, notes:

> The Carter administration set a goal of deriving 20 percent of U.S. energy needs from renewables. . . . By 1986, the Reagan administration had gutted the research and development budgets for renewable energy . . . and eliminated tax breaks for the deployment of wind turbines and solar technologies—recommitting the nation to reliance on cheap but polluting fossil fuels, often from foreign suppliers.

Of course, extensive public relations campaigns supporting fossil fuels, and the people who are wealthy because of these polluting industries, have spent millions on social media advertising alone to ensure that the general public does not understand the gravity of the problems. (See more in the "Banning Fossil Fuel Ads" section.) Interestingly, fossil fuel industries around the world continue to receive massive subsidies despite billions in profits.

HOW DO WE PROCEED?

At this point, we have probably heard the alarming news about our climate crisis. Perhaps we have even witnessed climate-related disturbances in our areas. My daughter, who works in Europe, for instance, was visiting Athens, Greece, when the city experienced unprecedented, dangerously high temperatures. But what exactly is climate change and how do we address it?

According to the U.S. Environmental Protection Agency (EPA), the gases that trap heat in the atmosphere —like a heavy blanket—are called greenhouse gases. Carbon dioxide, or CO_2, is the primary greenhouse gas emitted from human activities and accounts for 79 percent of all US greenhouse gas emissions. The EPA states, "The main human activity that emits CO_2 is the combustion of fossil fuels (**coal, natural gas, and oil**) for energy and transportation." Fossil fuels used for our transportation, to generate our electricity, and in our industrial processes are resulting in catastrophic climate problems. As such, "The most effective way to reduce CO_2 emissions is to reduce fossil fuel consumption."

When working to reduce fossil fuel consumption, it's important to note that there's a difference between "zero" and "net zero" greenhouse gas emissions. Zero means not producing any carbon dioxide. The total amount of green-house gases emitted by a group, industry, or person is referred to as a carbon footprint. A zero-carbon footprint is the aim. For example, if we use solar-powered lights, they will not produce any carbon emissions, resulting in a zero-carbon footprint. Net zero, on the other hand, means balancing the carbon produced with the amount that is captured. Buying carbon offsets when we fly in airplanes —which are then used to plant trees—is an example of net zero because the airplane's fossil fuel still continues to produce carbon in the atmosphere. In terms of carbon emissions, the best solutions are those that do not burn fossil fuels—in other words, zero greenhouse gas emissions.

The UCAR Center for Science Education, a teaching resource for educators and the general public, explains that there are two main ways to reduce greenhouse gas levels. First, stop emitting greenhouse gases into the air (i.e., fossil fuel consumption). Second, increase the Earth's ability to pull greenhouse gases out of the air. We can do the latter by protecting our forests and oceans, planting trees, and using farming methods that keep living roots (like cover crops) in the ground year-round.

Everyone—individuals, governments, schools, religious institutions, nonprofit organizations, and businesses—can take steps toward creating healthy, sustainable living on our Earth home. It would help enormously if instead of arguing about solutions (or even IF the problems exist), we began collectively doing our part to adopt a variety of beneficial actions.

Greenpeace, an international organization dedicated to preventing environmental abuses, has excellent information on sustainable climate solutions. Per Greenpeace, some key solutions we can adopt to mitigate climate change include:

- Keep fossil fuels (coal, oil, and gas) in the ground.
- Use renewable energy sources (solar, wind, hydropower, geothermal). We must get away from our dependence on fossil fuels.
- Reduce our carbon footprint. We need more walking and bicycle paths, mass public transit using clean sources of energy, and energy-efficient buildings, and we need to eliminate fossil fuels for vehicle and airplane travel.
- Preserve old-growth forests, plant trees, and create more green spaces.
- Eat more plant-based foods and convert to sustainable agricultural practices.
- Reduce consumption. Reuse items. Recycle.
- Reduce our use of plastics, which are made from fossil fuels.

All of these necessary measures assume that businesses are willing to voluntarily enact sustainable practices, even if legislation does not provide incentives—or suffer the already tangible consequences for failing to do so. In my experience, as someone who years ago worked as an attorney in employment discrimination law, it's better to have policies in place that protect people from harm than to assume that businesses will voluntarily avoid (or correct) harmful actions. By the same token, a plethora of innovative, entrepreneurial, eco-friendly businesses—and people who want to protect our Earth home—would greatly benefit from ecologically sound policies and clean-energy incentives. These environmentally friendly businesses are the ones we want to support.

One crucial thing we absolutely must do, as voters and as consumers, is to let elected officials and business leaders know that we want them to enact Earth-friendly measures in order to mitigate the threats from climate change. We need to ensure our local communities are healthy places to live and that our Earth home is protected. Meeting that goal will require all of us!

Given the climate disruptions we are already witnessing, I should mention that there are discussions about whether we can obtain the needed carbon reductions in time. For that reason, some people may take a nihilistic view regarding our ability to tackle climate change. But throwing our hands up in despair never solves anything—nor does ignoring the problem or attacking the people who are advocating for desired changes. Pessimism is not my approach to life and is definitely not my attitude toward tough situations. I have faith in our ability to address our environmental challenges, and I prefer to spend my time seeking solutions.

Admittedly, working to solve our ecological problems feels daunting at times. We know the issues are grave. We feel overwhelmed because we care. We want to save ourselves, our loved ones, and our global family from environmental calamities. While doing research for this book, I found myself assessing my own risks and the risks to people I love who live in various locations throughout the world. For poor and marginalized communities, the deadly consequences of our climate crisis are even more pronounced. But wealth and status will not save anyone if human civilization becomes sick with poisons, and the Earth is no longer able to support human life. The planet will survive, but we will not.

It's human nature to feel secure with the familiar, even when the familiar becomes detrimental to our well-being. It's also not uncommon to feel fearful when facing big changes. Yet, it's also human nature to want to help when we understand what's at stake. We are a resilient species, and we are capable of making healthy adjustments. Like the twelve-step programs mentioned in the Introduction, awareness is a fundamental first step. Succumbing to hopelessness is not a viable option if we want to create healthy, thriving communities for future generations.

With that in mind, I will begin this day where I am, at Saint Mary-of-the Woods. I will take a deep breath. I will meditate.

Pausing for a moment, I hear a train whistle somewhere in the distance. I close my eyes while envisioning what it would be like to travel across the United States from the East Coast to the West Coast or from the Northern states to the Southern states in comfortable, fast, inexpensive trains operated using clean energy, perhaps with comfortable sleeper cars and nutritious meals. What would it be like to have more bicycle and walking paths; to see numerous apartments, houses, businesses, and government buildings with solar panels and/or green rooftops; and to have flowering native plants across our landscapes, with organic vegetable gardens and fruit tree orchards available for the community? What would it be like to see an abundance of trees *everywhere*? What would it be like to see children playing in rivers, streams, and lakes that are safe enough to drink from?

Can we envision this future where our air is clean, our water is not polluted, our food is wholesome, and we are happier because we are healthier?

WALKING AN ANCIENT SPIRAL

Putting on my winter coat, gloves, scarf, and hiking boots, I head outside to survey my surroundings at Saint Mary-of-the-Woods. With a brightly shining sun, the weather is warm for January. I take off my heavy scarf and carry it. I am overdressed and overheating. The lack of snow worries me because it seems odd. I recall watching my children when they were young—during wintry January snow days in the Midwest—building snowmen, digging snow fort tunnels, and sledding down the snow-covered hillside at a neighborhood park. I hope those memories don't become relics of the past. What would an absence of snow mean for our water supplies? What would it mean for our survival?

The footpath I begin traveling this morning is more farmland than woods. I say hello to some horses in the field—also in their winter jackets—and stop by a fenced-in area to watch some chickens wandering around. Farther along, I come to alpacas. Given my aviator hat with dark, fake fur that covers both my forehead and the sides of my cheeks, I'm guessing I look like a long-lost kin to the alpacas, who stare quizzically at me. But soon, they go back to ignoring me as they continue their grazing.

After greeting these fine hosts, I walk on until I come upon a labyrinth in a lovely courtyard. I am thrilled. A labyrinth is not a maze; it is a circular path that leads to the center and then back out. As I walk the labyrinth in the crisp winter air under the bright overhead sun, I ask that this writing project be guided by Spirit. I ask for help in releasing my fears so that I may walk more steadily in faith, guided as I go.

I'm alone on the labyrinth and haven't seen anyone so far today. Feeling a bit lonely, I look around and observe that I am surrounded by trees—never truly alone among these giant friends. While following the winding path, I glance down and see faint shoe prints in the gravel of someone who has walked here before me. A bit later, I notice small paw prints. Perhaps a dog, raccoon, coyote, or deer also crossed this way.

As I slowly make my way along the ancient spiral pathways, I reflect on the life of Jesus, since his image and the story of his Crucifixion are found in statues placed throughout the grounds. A man who preached of love and spoke of a just world for all—especially the poor and downtrodden—was killed for his efforts to bring about a more compassionate humanity through his message of God's love. Nevertheless, his teachings have endured long past his death. If he were here today, his message would no doubt include love of our Earth because it is the poor who suffer most when our Earth home is damaged. Jesus knew the hungry should be fed. He knew that to love one another meant to be generous of heart and kind in spirit to all who are suffering. Of course, those views cost him his life. Powerful men do not like the idea of change when it means giving up control of what they perceive to be valuable.

Greta Thunberg, who stepped forward at age sixteen to voice concern for a planet and people in peril, was likewise vilified by men in power for conveying the critical message that we need to take care of our Earth home before it's too late. I read her speeches last night, and she repeats the same message again and again: the experts agree that we need to cut greenhouse gases in accordance with the scientists' findings in the Paris Climate Agreement. (The Paris Climate Agreement is an international treaty that commits most of the world's governments to address climate change. The goal is to limit the world's temperature increase to 1.5°C). Greta refers people to the world's scientists who have studied climate change. The studies show that, by far, the largest greenhouse gas emissions are coming from China and the United States. As she says, people in poor countries have the most to lose, and the leaders in the richest countries are failing to act.

As I walk the labyrinth, I wonder why humans are so intent on arguing with each other and vilifying people who speak up, instead of thanking them for caring so passionately about the welfare of humankind and the well-being of our shared Earth home.

Aren't all faith traditions—such as Christianity, Judaism, Hinduism, Buddhism, Paganism, and other world religions—trying to teach us to love one another and be good stewards of our shared Earth home?

I worry that I don't know enough to write a book about caring for our Earth. But then I think about Greta and the teachings of Jesus. I don't have to know everything to care. I can learn from the science experts. I can share what I'm learning. And I can do my part to contribute as best as I am able to. If a sixteen-year-old girl from Sweden can speak up for saving the planet, surely the rest of us can at least assist in those efforts.

Greta would say, "Listen to the scientists." Jesus would say, "If any of your brethren suffer, you suffer." Judaism would say, "We must be repairers of the world." Earth-based spiritual leaders would add, "Listen to Mother Earth, the water, the wind, and the trees." Buddhist monks would remind us, "Be mindful of each moment, bringing compassionate awareness to our thoughts, words, and deeds." Saint Mother Theodore Guerin, foundress of Saint Mary-of-the-Woods, would say, "Spend some time in the woods listening to God."

WHO WAS SAINT MOTHER THEODORE GUERIN?

After exiting the labyrinth, I wander to a log cabin where Mother Theodore Guerin (born Anne-Therese Guerin in 1798) stayed upon her arrival here. It is a small, plain, one-room replica of the original cabin. Next, I head toward the church.

It seems fitting that I visited the cabin before making my way to the church, not unlike the nuns who arrived here with Mother Theodore Guerin before any buildings were prepared for them. As I approach the church, I see a row of vultures perched high on the building's ledge, one with its wings spread out while basking in the sun's warm rays. I suppose even vultures, creatures not considered appealing by most people, dutifully serve their role here on Earth—scavenging from and cleaning up dead carcasses and helping to prevent the spread of diseases to other animals—regardless of the lack of gratitude shown by humans.

Once inside the building, I make my way to the chapel. I hear organ music from someone rehearsing in the balcony. Like the vultures, I find a seat in the sun, which shines radiantly through a stained-glass window. I, too, bask for a bit in the peaceful ambience, saying a silent prayer, again asking for guidance. Then, I head to the room where Saint Mother Theodore Guerin's story is displayed with placards, images, and various items from her life. There, I see her writing desk where she avidly wrote her letters and in her journals. I learn that she is the first saint from Indiana. While reading her story, I determine that this is the woman I want guiding me on this project: a strong woman who loved the woods, who built orphanages and schools for girls, and who suffered as a young girl with the loss of her father and the death of two brothers. Throughout her life, she devoted herself steadfastly to the service of others.

I feel I have found a kindred spirit to lead me forward on the task at hand. Though I am not a scientist or scholar, I realize even more profoundly that we don't have to be experts to do our part in this world. We can let providence guide us and let our skills be put to good use.

Each time I feel uncertain about the way forward, I am going to read and re-read Saint Mother Theodore Guerin's quote:

"We are not called upon to do all the good that is possible, but only that which we can do."

MY HUMBLE ABODE AT BAILLY HERMITAGE

On the walk back to my hermitage, I stop by the White Violet Farm Store, where I buy organic spinach, dill dressing, and sourdough bread. In winter, the sun begins its descent here around 5:00 p.m., the darkness making it seem much later than it is.

When I return to my retreat hermitage, I prepare dinner. I add dried cranberries to my spinach, pesto to my bread, and heat up a bowl of soup. I've never had a better meal. Food doesn't have to be an expensive, MasterChef-dazzling gourmet feast: fresh wholesome ingredients make all the difference, especially after walking in the brisk outdoor air.

As I'm eating, I notice a framed sign on the wall: "Welcome to Bailly Hermitage." Sister Mary Cecilia Bailly, I learn, wrote the first biography of Mother Theodore Guerin, *The Life of Mother Theodore*, which served as evidence for her becoming a saint. I am excited to be staying in a retreat house named after a woman who was also a writer.

A welcome folder explains that the Bailly Hermitage house was made from recycled materials. Wood was donated for the biomass boiler (a heating system that uses natural/non-fossil fuel resources to create heat for the premises), and recycled wood was used for framing the building. Flooring came from truck beds, and wood from an old warehouse was used for the kitchen cabinetry, window frames, and baseboards. The windows came from a company whose buyers had returned custom-made windows, and the bathroom flooring was made using materials from a Habitat for Humanity ReStore warehouse.

Interestingly, the toilet paper and paper towels at my hermitage are from a company called Right Choice. According to its website, the items are biodegradable, recyclable, and chlorine-free. The company policy states that it seeks to use sustainable energy practices in its buildings, transportation, and packaging. The Natural Resources Defense Council likewise publishes a toilet paper sustainability scorecard for such businesses. In our household, we purchase from companies that have received an A rating on the scorecard.

Each small thing we do, multiplied by the actions of millions of people everywhere, does make a difference. Organic local food, for instance, means reduced pesticide use and less reliance on fossil fuel for transportation. Local organic gardens also ensure food security and better nutrition. Better nutrition results in healthier bodies and fewer medical costs. It's all connected: healthy choices, a healthy planet, and healthy humans.

Before heading to bed, I type up the day's nature chronicles and begin reading another of my environmental books. It's quiet here, and I am content.

Today was a good day.

WATER IS A SACRED GIFT

I woke up this morning to find a light snow dusting the landscape here in the woods. It's picturesque on the tree branches and over the lake's surface—even more appreciated after reading about the water shortages across the planet and the melting glaciers. We need snow!

I spent some time reading *Blue Covenant* last night by Maude Barlow, cofounder of the Blue Planet Project. Her straightforward message that everyone should have access to clean drinking water seems obvious. But many places around the globe, including the Western United States, are facing droughts and water scarcity issues. We have extensive water pollution problems as well. At the time of this writing, Indiana tops the list with more polluted rivers and streams than any state in the United States, according to a 2022 Environmental Integrity Project report. Of course, everyone in Michigan is aware of the disastrous Flint health crisis with lead contamination in the drinking water. The water disaster in Flint—a predominantly Black community with high levels of poverty—is just one example of the environmental health disparities for minority communities living in low-income neighborhoods.

In her book, Barlow also discusses the terrible consequences when private companies treat water as a commodity to own and, thereby, profit from its sale: taking water from poor countries, buying up lakefront properties, or bringing in ships to drain water from the lakes in order to sell it. As Barlow points out, no one should ever have to pay for bottled water, which further adds to the plastic pollution problem. (See more in "A Few Words about Plastics" section.) While it's true that in Flint, free drinking water in plastic bottles was brought in to help in that emergency situation. Barlow argues that bottled water for emergencies should not be a for-profit business venture. Rather, those industries polluting our drinking water should be paying us, the public, whenever our tap water is not drinkable and, per Barlow, safe drinking water for emergencies such as that in Flint should be operated and distributed by the government like in any other disaster relief program.

Water is a sacred gift, flowing down mountains and through valleys, replenishing the Earth and its aquifers (the underground layers and rock areas that contain water) and bringing life to plants and all living beings. As Indigenous Water Protectors (an Indigenous-led movement to safeguard Earth's water from harm) remind us: we come from water, and we are water. Water is life itself. Without water, we perish. Just as we do not own the sun, the sky, or the ocean tides, we do not own water. Instead, we should give thanks for the gift of life water brings to all living beings on Mother Earth.

WALKING AMONG GIANTS

Today is my last full day at Saint Mary-of-the-Woods. A brilliant orange sunrise in the east appears especially vibrant against the stark white landscape. Watching the sun rise in the central region of the Midwest is not quite the panoramic vision of an early morning sunrise over oceans, lakes, and mountaintops. Here, winter's rising sun is a momentary brilliance that promises nothing, with outdoor temperatures at 18°F today and a gray overcast sky. But daylight does gradually arrive, even in the midst of winter and irrespective of our hopes, dreams, or despairs.

During my morning meditation, I open my eyes for a moment and glance out the window just as a red-tail hawk lands high in a tree across the frozen lake. I see the glimpses of red as the hawk ruffles its tail feathers; it's barely visible with a brownish body that blends well with the tree limbs. Once spotted, I can view the hawk, a large bird, even from my distance inside the hermitage. I hope to have the hawk's vision for this writing project, as well as the wisdom of bobcats, bears, beavers, and other creatures of the land, sky, and sea. Our planet Earth is so exquisite when untainted by man's misguided hunger for power. The Earth will likely survive without us; it is we who need clean air, fresh water, and healthy soil, and it is we who harm all of creation—including ourselves—when we fail to practice good stewardship of this glorious Eden bestowed upon us during our brief sojourn here.

As the hawk suddenly flies off, coasting over the lake, I realize there are two of them; the other hawk is perched on a lower branch. Are they a pair? I wait a moment and then yes, the second hawk follows in flight, both landing on tree branches farther away. Soon, they depart beyond my view.

After my meditation, I eat my breakfast of cooked oats and then sit down to enjoy a cup of tea. Yesterday, I was reading *A Sand County Almanac*, written by Aldo Leopold. Leopold has a true gift for observation of the natural world. I can see why the book is a nature classic; he is a skilled naturalist, birder, historian, and storyteller. Leopold puts forth a land ethic, with the argument that living things in nature have intrinsic value regardless of any economic benefit to humans. I agree wholeheartedly with that premise. He also mentions heating his home with wood chopped from an old tree struck by lightning on his property. While that source of heat might have been feasible at the time—*A Sand County Almanac* was published posthumously in 1949—it doesn't seem especially helpful at present. With so few forested areas left in our urban landscapes, fallen trees provide habitat for wildlife that don't have any safe places left to go. A lot of people also don't live on acreage, nor have the skills to chop trees, myself included.

Renewable energy, such as solar, may not have been a viable option in the 1940s. But as we know now, transitioning to renewable energy, along with tree plantings, are critical elements in addressing climate change. In places like Haiti, where they reduce wood to charcoal for use as cooking fuel, deforestation has resulted in terrible devastation with few trees left to act as barriers to the intense floodwaters that rush forth from hurricanes and tropical storms.

Change, as they say, is the only constant. In terms of human evolution, it is required if we are to survive. I sit down at the computer and begin typing: Earth book, draft one. This book will undoubtedly see many drafts. Let's hope the numerous changes we each make on this life journey move us forward, together, toward something splendid and worthwhile while there is still time.

As midday approaches, I step outside onto the snow-dusted porch. With the cold afternoon air, my walk outdoors will be shorter today than on preceding days. After bundling up, I head toward the woods.

A sign at the trailhead explains the importance of trees in providing oxygen and taking in carbon. Of course, trees also serve an important part in providing habitat to birds, bees, squirrels, owls, bats, copious insects, and other living creatures. Each tree is a home. A number of trees together form a community. Do we consider all the lives in that community before we build roads, businesses, and houses? Have we ever said, "Thank you," as we walk among the trees that supply our cooling shade in the summer, protect our ground from erosion, and offer astonishing beauty all year long? At one time, people, known as the Druids, worshipped trees. To revere the old-growth forests was perhaps an ancient way of honoring the indispensable role of trees in our survival, as well as the welfare of so many crea-tures here on Earth.

Walking among these lovely giant friends is a pleasant way to spend my last day at Saint Mary-of-the-Woods. Trees serve as a gentle reminder: let your roots go deep, let your branches reach high, and let yourself be open to the beautiful gifts of hummingbirds, hawks, eagles, blue jays, robins, wrens, woodpeckers, warblers, chickadees, mockingbirds, crows, and all the winged beings bringing joyful songs to each new day.

Tonight, numerous creatures will make their beds in these woodlands, and birds will roost high in the tree tops, perhaps lulled to sleep by the hoots of a great horned owl.

SUN SALUTATIONS

This morning, I prepare to return home. I'm going to meditate and remind myself: the world is full of marvelous sights and simple pleasures found in nature. Right now, a rose-colored sky presents a peaceful respite where I can take a moment to breathe, ask for guidance, and release—again and again—my need to control. I will journey home grounded in stillness and in faith. I will take with me the lessons from the woods.

After my meditation, I see sunlight beaming on the trees near the water, a dazzling, iridescent glow. Those trees soak up the soft light, facing the sun full-on, as though in awe themselves of the resplendent bright light rising before them. I wonder how our lives would transform if we were taught to pay homage for a few moments each morning to the sun, giving thanks for the life-giving force it brings equally to all: the trees, birds, humans, plants, and an array of life in our lakes, streams, rivers, and oceans.

It's enormously restoring to set aside time to mindfully breathe, reflect, and observe our natural environments. Nature reminds us to live in harmony with our Earth home. Through nature, we learn how to appreciate clear waters flowing through our streams, how to feel the ground beneath our feet, how to gather food from the land, how to observe the sky above our heads, and how to notice the crisp wind on our cheeks, a fallen tree at the lake's edge, or a squirrel leaping from branch to branch, adeptly defying gravity.

When I glance toward the back deck, I detect sparkling sunlight glistening across the snow, each tiny sparkle a colorful prism of ice and sunlight. A child standing here with me to see this snow-covered porch as it magically shimmers in the sunlight would be full of glee and wonder at the miracle of it! Such amazing splendor in the small observed details of the present moment!

Thich Nhat Hanh, one of my favorite Buddhist teachers, dedicated his entire life to teaching us: *Breathe. Slow down. Pay attention to this moment.*

It's a gift I now pass on to you. Try it.

Take a few slow, deep breaths. Observe this moment, giving it your full attention. Step outdoors if you are able to. Look up at the sky, the clouds, the surrounding landscape.

See what wonders await you this day.

CHAPTER TWO

URBAN LANDSCAPES

"To pay attention, this is our endless and proper work."

— MARY OLIVER, POET

RETURNING HOME

Upon arriving home from my retreat, I notice a light snow on the frozen ground alongside a few brown grassy patches. Our winter weather has gone from 60°F to 1°F in the span of a week. These wide temperature swings are stressful to plants and living creatures on multiple levels. For example, a sudden change in temperature—warm during the day and then freezing at night—can cause the outer layer of a tree trunk to crack. Like humans, trees that become stressed are more susceptible to opportunistic diseases and, in some cases, to premature death. Anyone with indoor houseplants knows how sensitive plants can be to too much watering, not enough water, too much cold, or too much heat. It's no different for the wide variety of organisms living on our planet.

As I head indoors, a large spider in a corner of the ceiling seems startled by my entrance. The spider and her web always serve to remind me that everything is connected. I tell myself to stay open to what comes this day and to be mindful of the words I weave. No need to chase the spider, or capture it, or squash it! The spider is not harming me. We can co-exist in this warm interior space, safe from the elements, and, in return, the spider eats other unwelcome insects, though I'm not sure what the spider finds to eat during winter. All the same, I welcome this spider and perhaps she welcomes me.

After unpacking, I settle in for the day. The wind outside is whipping against the windows. It sounds foreboding. It is the type of day when staying inside under blankets is preferable to venturing out. I prepare a cup of tea and make myself comfortable on the couch. While drinking my tea, my daughter sends me a text asking if I can get her a container of pepper spray. Yesterday, a man shoved a young woman onto the New York City subway train tracks, killing the woman. My eldest daughter, who lives in New York City, rides that subway to work. Of course, I agree to get her the pepper spray. When my step-father died, my mother had an alarm system installed in her house and had a handgun placed in the drawer of her bedside table. This is not a book that advocates the use of violence. It is, however, an acknowledgment that women feel the need to take drastic measures for self-protection and self-preservation.

As mentioned earlier, I believe there is a link between the violence against women and the violence inflicted against Mother Earth. Are some men not regarding women as living, breathing, intelligent humans worthy of respect and love? Are some people not viewing Mother Earth as a living, breathing organism worthy of respect, reverence, and love? When did we stop listening to the Earth and to the women across the globe? I should add, this violence isn't directed *only* against women. It's also violence targeted against Blacks, Indigenous Peoples, immigrants, migrants, LGBTQ individuals, and the poor, along with other ethnic, religious, and culturally marginalized groups. In addition, it's violence against whales in the oceans, polar bears in the Artic, and elephants across distant lands. It's violence against our forests and the creatures depending on those trees for habitat. It's deadly violence against all that we love—and for what purpose?

Power? Control? Hatred? Greed?

The mighty oak outside my window seems to say:

"Do you remember the ancient ways of people who honored nature? Do you remember when women were revered as givers-of-life with Goddess temples and female deities? Do you remember the joy and strength of people who gather together to sing, dance, and celebrate life?"

A BACKYARD HAVEN

Perhaps one way to begin caring for our Earth home is by honoring the spaces we currently inhabit. My yard doesn't have a deck, lake, or woods, but it does have mature oak trees and towering pines, along with several saplings that my husband and I planted. We are located in an urban neighborhood in Indianapolis and are fortunate to have racial, religious, and ethnic diversity where we live. Our backyard looks out on two of our neighbors' yards. There are no fences, so the green space appears larger when combined with the others.

In the spring, I plant my herbs—basil, cilantro, thyme, rosemary—and a couple of tomato plants in raised beds. The perennial lemon balm, spearmint, peppermint, chives, and lavender bloom each spring as well. I have also planted purple coneflowers, hostas, wild ginger, bee balms, black-eyed Susans, milkweeds, bluebells, and an heirloom lilac bush that is now eight feet tall. Some of our native plants, such as the purple asters, were given to us by Keep Indianapolis Beautiful, a local nonprofit. A volunteer pokeweed's dark red berries delight the birds in autumn, and an abundance of clover, violets, and bright yellow dandelions make our yard glorious in the spring and summer.

When my husband and I moved into this house, the entire backyard and front yard consisted of grass and dry, bare dirt beneath the trees. The grass presents an unsafe landscape for chipmunks, rabbits, birds, and other small creatures who have no nearby cover while traveling from place to place in search of food. It took a lot of work to create our native flowerbeds. I had to dig through hard clay to remove the grass. The clay ground is the result of builders who removed the topsoil when building these houses. So, the first step involved getting the ground healthy by adding back the missing organic material that was removed with the topsoil.

We moved into our house in July, and I brought a few native plants with me from my prior location, which had high organic soil (almost peatlike) from the previous owner's years of composting. I tried planting some of those flowers at my present location, and they were so wilted and near death that my daughters scoffed at the idea of me trying to create a flowerbed in our grassy, clay landscape. One of the neighbors also thought it odd how hard I was working to get rid of the grass and to dig through the hard clay, telling me that I looked like a dog out there digging. (I think he may have been more accustomed to landscaping crews doing the labor for homeowners.)

While not all the flowers made it through that first summer, our yard now has a "Pollinator Habitat" sign amid the numerous flowering plants, and neighbors occasionally stop by to ask about the sign and our native plants. We have mulch around the trees, a wood brush pile that serves as wildlife habitat, a picnic table, and a swing we hung from a large oak branch. We also planted raspberries and blackberries. For a small neighborhood plot, we have done well to make our yard pollinator-friendly and wildlife habitat-friendly. With the picnic table, trees, and swing, it's a peaceful, park-like oasis with natural cooling shade during the summer.

With our extensive flowerbeds, we have less mowing now in the summer. Recently, we bought a battery-powered lawn mower for the remaining grass that does need mowing. The dried leaves that we rake in the autumn are added to the flowerbeds, serving as mulch and protection for winter. We never bag our leaves; that would be a waste of decomposed matter for other living creatures and would add to the plastic pollution problems. The organic mulch and deep roots of the native plants we used to replace the grass help to absorb excess rainwater and continue to nourish the soil. As a result, our habitat-friendly yard has resulted in better rain absorption (rather than runoff into the streets), a variety of bird species, and more wildlife, such as an occasional opossum, rabbit, raccoon, fox, coyote, or deer stopping by to gather food and seek shelter. I feel fortunate to count wildlife among my most treasured and welcome neighbors.

Over the years, numerous birds have come to visit: orioles, blue jays, mourning doves, cardinals, goldfinches, house finches, grosbeaks, Carolina wrens, brown thrashers, robins, Northern flickers, grackles, Eastern towhees, hummingbirds, bluebirds, tanagers, tufted titmouse, owls, pileated woodpeckers, and more!

We have a diversity of trees as well. The redbud, dogwood, and maple trees, along with a tulip tree (Indiana's state tree), are all volunteer seedlings that we nurtured by weeding around them or by moving them to areas where they will flourish and grow into mature trees. We have a sweetgum tree out front that has dropped excessive amounts of gumballs this winter. Perhaps that tree is stressed? I've read that trees may produce more seeds when triggered by environmental stressors like high temperatures or drought. As a result of the emerald ash borer, native to Asia and brought to Michigan in 2002, millions of ash trees in the United States—and many ash trees in our neighborhood—died. That's why it is a good idea to have a variety of trees and plants in neighborhoods and in wooded areas: the diversity of species keeps the wooded habitat alive if for some reason one species is eliminated. While our neighbors lost most of their ash trees, the neighborhood as a whole has retained a host of diverse trees.

We don't spray our yard with chemical fertilizers or pesticides, knowing that those poisons seep into the ground. Last June, I was walking around my neighborhood and saw a baby mole on its back in the middle of the road, struggling to survive. I had never seen a baby mole before; it was so vulnerable and very cute. Likely, the lawns nearby were sprayed with chemicals. Not long ago, a large number of bird deformities and bird deaths took place across the United States, and everyone was advised to take down their bird feeders. One theory for the unexplained bird deaths is that the cicadas, emerging from the ground and then eaten by the birds, contained too much pesticides that they had absorbed from the soil. I don't know if scientists ever definitively discovered the cause of the bird deaths, but it certainly doesn't bode well for humans when other living creatures become ill, die off, or go extinct. Of course, as mentioned previously, Rachel Carson's book, *Silent Spring*, predicted as much from the decades of accumulated poisons we put into the air, water, and land.

MEDICINAL PLANTS

When I was pregnant, I had a passion for learning about the healing properties of plants. Herbal books are a wonderful resource for gaining information about natural plant remedies, such as echinacea, mint, lemon balm, lavender, chamomile, and so on. Keep in mind that some herbs can only be used topically while others are safe to ingest. It's always a good idea to check with plant experts if you are unsure.

One time when my daughter was young and got a belly ache at school, the school nurse gave her a hard peppermint candy to soothe her stomach until I arrived, as the school couldn't dispense medicine. It makes sense that peppermint growing in the yard can be brewed for tea to help settle the stomach. Similarly, when I was growing up in Michigan, parents often gave their children ginger ale to drink for an upset stomach. Soda pop is not something I drink or ever gave my children, but a bit of ginger root is easy enough to use in teas. For a toothache, some people use ground clover mixed with water to numb their gums until they can get to the dentist.

A traditional doctor in the United States isn't necessarily trained or knowledgeable about remedies outside of Western medicine. Nevertheless, people have used a variety of healing plants long before pharmaceutical companies existed. That is not to say that Western medicine and pharmaceuticals aren't serving a necessary, oftentimes lifesaving, purpose. We can use the best of our combined knowledge—science, herbal, and Indigenous wisdom—for our optimal health. (See more in the "Indigenous Wisdom" chapter.) These different areas of knowledge should not be disregarded. I am a spiritual, intuitive person who prefers natural remedies where appropriate, but I married a biologist and definitely appreciate—and utilize—scientific expertise. My husband and I complement each other because we are open to learning from one another. We also both enjoy learning from people with knowledge beyond our own.

A LONG, GRAY WINTER

A light gentle snow is falling today, barely discernable against a white sky with no sun. In the Midwest, we've had occasional cold temperatures but not a snowy winter wonderland. In fact, we didn't get any snow at all for Christmas. I miss the gleeful abandon of children playing outdoors in snowsuits and heavy boots as they trudge up the hill and then sled down, again and again, with cheerful squeals. My youngest daughter, who lives in Europe for work, went skiing in the Swiss Alps over the holidays, and she reported that most of the main slopes were closed due to a lack of snow accumulation. Meanwhile, areas out west in the United States are getting hit with unprecedented ice storms and blizzards, while locations across the globe that depend on snow for winter sports remain green and brown. If you watch nature documentaries, you can't miss the devastation these weather shifts are causing for the local wildlife as well.

I try to go walking each day, but the walk is not pleasant when the temperatures drop too low and the wind is icy. The past couple of days, I didn't go out at all because of the extreme cold. The only upside is that the gray skies do prompt me to sit at my desk and write, though I have to work hard to push through the sense of hopelessness that can arise when listening to the news of global weather-related calamities and resulting deaths.

Two pileated woodpeckers with bright red heads and striking black feathers land on the tree outside my office window, stopping by as though to say, *"Keep at it,"* while they, too, go about their work of seeking nourishment amid the cold.

HEAVY RAINS

I hear birds in the yard chirping today. It's raining and 50°F, so the robins are enjoying their splashing baths in the backyard puddles. Small lakes are rapidly forming in ditches and in neighboring yards. I'm glad our mulched areas are absorbing the excess rainwater, whereas the grass lawns nearby have large pools of water. Newscasters are warning of a severe winter storm front headed our way. Maybe the birds are enjoying the warmer temperatures before the freeze comes. I also notice what looks like a baby squirrel: tiny and gray. Do squirrels have babies in winter? Do weather patterns alter wildlife reproductive cycles?

We have warm weather followed by freezing. Followed by warmth. We know something is wrong. Flooding problems are occurring across the planet, sometimes even when the sky is sunny and blue. I experienced this type of unexpected street flooding during a visit to Miami when helping my eldest daughter move into her apartment for her optometry externship. My Uber driver was attempting to drive through a flash flood, talking in Spanish on his cell phone, cursing, while I stared out the car window at the torrent of water rushing past the vehicle. Eventually, we were able to pull over to an area under a hotel awning,

away from the flooded streets, but I doubt his car—which
is most likely the source of his livelihood—will ever be the
same. It was a frightening experience, and I am grateful
that he was able to navigate us safely out of the rushing
floodwaters.

Downpours with catastrophic flooding have occurred
across the United States in places such as New York, California, Vermont, Nevada, Massachusetts, Maine, Texas,
and so on, with loss of lives and property—likewise in
Kentucky, where heavy rains created terrible flooding that
washed away homes and people in its path, including
school-age children. In Michigan, where my mother lives,
the lake shoreline beaches have eroded due to rising water
levels—in some cases, leaving no sandy beach whatsoever.
The same with devastating floods in Libya, Spain, India,
Italy, Greece, Turkey, Japan, Mexico, Brazil, Hong Kong,
Bulgaria, and elsewhere around the world. Almost daily,
we read about flooding tragedies, along with hurricanes,
ravaging coastal regions and islands. Not long ago, we
experienced some of the worst hurricane damage ever in
the United States along the Florida coast.

Despite the dangers from flooding, commercial
building projects and housing developments continue to
raze urban forests at alarming rates, which means when
the heavy rains arrive, the water has nowhere to go. Often,
fields, prairies, and wetlands get converted into buildings
or cement parking lots. So, of course, rainwater floods
onto the roads and into the neighborhoods. Ongoing
development results in a loss of deep-rooted trees and
deep-rooted native plants that would help absorb the
excess downpour. (See more in "A Love of Trees"
chapter.)

I have witnessed firsthand the annihilation of urban
forests to put in expensive housing and commercial business developments. The old-growth trees get decimated,

along with the flowers, plants, and millions of living creatures. Sometimes, developers plant a few young decorative trees around a newly constructed massive parking lot—as though that somehow makes up for the extensive eradication of mature trees and all the life forms dependent on those trees. When a Walmart was going up in a wooded area near my home, a good friend of mine went on a rescue-the-daffodils mission, digging up the bulbs before the ground was bulldozed. Where I live, most developers are not saving old-growth trees. They are not installing solar power on their buildings. They are not rehabilitating existing buildings to help blighted neighborhoods. Instead, they are in the business of making money regardless of the cost to life on our planet.

Destruction from flooding is the risk we face when people fail to keep natural habitats, such as forests, prairies, fields, and wetlands.

Eliminating our urban forests—which would otherwise lower air temperatures and store carbon—can also exacerbate the intensity and frequency of flooding brought about by climate change. A warmer atmosphere "holds and subsequently dumps more water," according to the Natural Resources Defense Council. Scientists indicate that extreme weather—heavy or prolonged rains, storm surges, sudden snowmelts, sea level rise, and other climate changes—can cause more flooding and increase the likelihood of more intense hurricanes. Unless we start doing things differently, these environmental disruptions are predicted to get worse. Per the Natural Resources Defense Council's website, "Heavy precipitation events are projected to increase (along with temperatures) . . . bringing as much as 50 percent more heavy rain by the end of this century."

Two critical questions we might wish to explore: How much lobbying power do developers hold over local politicians, and do these developers occupy positions on zoning boards? How might we rethink urban development to safeguard our wooded and natural areas, making our communities safer from flooding catastrophes?

FINALLY, SNOW!

It's February, and a winter storm blows across the land here with thick snow covering the rooftops and tree limbs. A brown squirrel scampers from branch to branch, not looking in the least disturbed. The snow is beautiful! I'm so happy that snowfall has finally arrived. Children are sledding, and the landscape seems brighter as the sun reflects off the snowy white surface. Deer tracks can be seen across the yard, along with rabbit and squirrel paw prints. Everything is blanketed in white.

Even though I am happy to see the arrival of snow, I still feel worried about our ability to make a lasting, positive difference in time, especially considering the magnitude of our climate change challenges. Often, the environmental problems we face as Earth stewards can seem insurmountable. All the same, I will trudge ahead doing what I can, hoping that promising changes will still emerge.

FEBRUARY RAINS

We're back to more rain today. The snow is melting as temperatures climb, with an expected high of 52°F. The rivers rise. The rain falls. I keep finding ants throughout the house, in February. Is that normal? According to a presentation I attended at the Environmental Resilience Institute, climate change is resulting in more rain at the wrong time. In other words, we get heavy rains in winter and spring but not enough rain during the active growing season when plants most need it. There are lots of depressing stats about the havoc climate change is causing.

On my walk yesterday, I saw an eagle and three hawks. I hope my nature chronicles bring better news soon.

My mother went to the emergency room last night—a urinary tract infection and kidney infection—which put her final chemotherapy temporarily on hold. Such infections are side effects of her cancer treatments. We are going to Michigan to visit her later this afternoon.

The year I dedicated to writing about nature is also the year my mother is fighting advanced lung cancer. She lives in a rural area in Michigan near Lake Huron, which is located on the east side of the mitten for those familiar with Michigan's map layout. I wonder how many people in her town have had cancer diagnoses. She has never been a cigarette smoker or alcohol drinker, and she does not live with anyone who smokes. She is physically active, and there is no family history of lung cancer. No one seems to know the cause. Then again, doctors who treat cancer aren't necessarily assessing exposure to environmental pollutants. We put so much energy into marching for a cure to cancer, but how much cancer funding goes into studying environmental causes and then working to eliminate those sources of pollution?

New York City, where my eldest daughter now lives, is 63°F today. In February! I feel sad. Some people are happy in winter for the warmer temperatures. But what about the increase in floods? What about the climate-related deaths of plants and wildlife? Do we think we will somehow escape that same fate if we continue on with business as usual? What about extreme summer heat waves and resulting human diseases due to an increase in fungi, mold, and more tropic-like sicknesses? What about the rapid rise in certain insect populations? For instance, according to an article published at the Yale School of

Environment, climate change has fueled the advance of bark beetles, which have ravaged hundreds of thousands of square miles of forest in the United States and Canada and from Europe to Siberia. Scientists are talking about adaptation and mitigation of damages—meaning it's too late for prevention? Perhaps humans will face the consequences of our own actions—whatever that looks like—while the Earth adjusts as needed, which may or may not include humans. Or maybe if we give our Earth home adequate time and space to heal, we will all benefit and, perhaps, someday thrive.

I pause to listen.

Birds are chirping. The rain has stopped.

I watch the tree branches sway in the breeze. I ask the sturdy oaks in my yard to help me not sink into despair.

I set my sight and my resolve on love. I acknowledge there is work to be done.

BECOMING QUIET WITHIN

A full moon is observable in the western morning sky, framed between the stark tree branches. A rising sun or bright shining moon always gives me hope. We're having a cold spell this morning with a temperature of 14°F.

A soft rosy hue appears overhead. Birds are singing before most humans have stirred from their slumber. I woke up at 6:00 a.m. It's peaceful in the early mornings when thoughts, movements, and activities for the upcoming day are at rest.

In this quiet space, gratitude for simple pleasures—warmth, coffee, friends, and family—rise into my awareness. Dried leaves dangle from the oak tree limbs, not letting go despite winter's cold winds. I have gratitude for the tall green pine trees in the midst of so much slate gray.

While spring remains far off, I know that buds—and vibrant new life—will eventually re-emerge.

At 7:45 a.m., the sun rises in this part of the world and a new day begins. Soon, traffic will pick up, along with emails, calls, texts, and social media communications; along with worries, illnesses, sorrows, and heartaches; along with celebrations, laughter, happiness, and joy. What path awaits us this day?

What do we hear when the Earth slumbers in winter, and we become quiet within, like the trees that stand sturdy against the cold? What do we hear when we breathe, slow down, and patiently wait for signs of spring?

Listen—to the caws, the high-pitched chirps, the drips of icicles dangling from the roof's edge.

While drinking my coffee, I happen to glance out my office window and see a fox running across the yard and then quickly disappearing from sight, perhaps hiding under the neighbor's deck. I've spotted coyotes in the neighborhood, but a fox sighting is much rarer. It is a gorgeous animal! During the pandemic shutdown, deer freely wandered our neighborhood streets. If we give animals space to roam and more nature-friendly habitat, we'd cohabitate better with wild things.

Maybe we should establish urban quiet times, like they do on lakes with designated no-wake zones and times. We could keep traffic off the roads during certain hours unless needed for emergencies. Or we could designate no-car areas so we could have safe spaces for animals, bicycles, and walking. European cities have done so, and some restaurant areas in the United States did so during the pandemic to allow for additional outdoor seating space.

Glancing outside, a bluebird unexpectedly perches on the wire that stretches over the yard. The small bird is only there a moment, but I am happy to see its soft blue hues in the winter landscape. The bluebird of happiness—it does bring joy with its appearance.

CITY PARKS

Heading over to Eagle Creek Park, one of the largest city parks in the United States with close to 4,000 acres, I decide to walk the trails this afternoon. Walking in the park is excellent exercise, and the park trees do so much to help our air quality. On top of producing clean air for us to breathe and lowering temperatures in summer so buildings don't have to use as much air conditioning, trees also absorb and store carbon, which, as previously mentioned, helps to mitigate climate change. Additionally, trees remove pollutants from the air. People who preserve and protect our local, state, and national parks, along with the individuals working at nonprofits focused on tree plantings —such as One Tree Planted, The Nature Conservancy, and the Arbor Day Foundation, to name a few—have my admiration. In fact, the individuals and organizations involved in park conservation are my heroes, not the men in expensive business suits who seem intent on destroying our Earth home.

Along the hiking trail, I see a heron at the end of a dock. Water is flowing in the middle of the lake despite the frozen shoreline and, consequently, the fish there are still accessible to the heron. As a morning person, it's harder for me to begin a hike this late in the day. But afternoon temperatures are warmer than early morning. Staying healthy is a priority, now more than ever because of my age and because of the enormous number of deaths we witnessed during the COVID-19 pandemic. Like all of nature, we are more resilient when we are physically well. I consider myself fortunate to have access to city, state, and national parks, though I do have to drive in order to reach them.

URBAN GARDENS AND FARMS

Years ago, I participated in community garden projects. One garden at a church I attended, which is located in an urban environment, served to connect the church community to its neighbors and supplied people with access to free, fresh, organic vegetables. Later, I had a plot in a neighborhood community garden where I had moved when my daughters were young.

When I was growing up, my family didn't garden because we had limited yard space and because my parents were busy working. So, it was useful as an adult for me to meet people with gardening skills who could share planting ideas. It was also a wonderful way to involve my children in the direct experience of learning where their food comes from. The neighbors got together for an occasional pitch-in to share home-cooked items from the garden, which allowed me to get to know people in the neighborhood. Being part of a gardening community was a fun, inexpensive, and educational activity. And I had fresh organic vegetables!

More recently, I met with Dr. Candace Corson, who has a passion for nutritional plant-based medicine. She encourages people to eat a variety of vegetables and fruits for improved health. Her small yard is a showcase of herbal plants, with almost every available space occupied by medicinal herbs. She also has Tower Gardens, both indoors and outdoors. These structures can be used indoors for growing plants year-round. Candace says Tower Gardens are especially beneficial for city dwellers who do not have large outdoor areas for garden plots. As she explains, Tower Gardens are vertical, so they don't require a lot of space, and they don't require soil, using instead aeroponics, which is a technology NASA uses.

Farmers' markets and community-led food cooperatives are another great way to obtain local fruits and vegetables. In some cities, these food items are available year-round, thanks to the use of greenhouses and hoop houses producing an array of fresh produce and extending the growing season. Food co-ops enable members to buy food in bulk, which can make fresh fruits and vegetables less expensive.

Urban farms on college campuses can also provide fresh produce to students and, in some cases, to the community. An excellent example is The Farm at Butler University in Indianapolis, a one-acre sustainable agricultural project managed by the Center for Urban Ecology and Sustainability. The Farm offers educational opportunities to the students and the community about sustainable agriculture and the local food system as well as providing local, organic food to the dining campus.

Farm-to-table restaurants are likewise a popular means for encouraging the consumption of food that is grown in a sustainable way. A favorite restaurant of mine is Public Greens, with its flagship location on a public greenway in Broad Ripple, a neighborhood in Indianapolis. Public Greens is an urban micro farm (small-scale farming), supplying produce, herbs, and edible flowers for the restaurant. Public Greens has a farmer/beekeeper and utilizes environmental sustainability measures throughout its business practices. In addition to fresh, locally grown ingredients, Public Greens' profits go to support The Patachou Foundation, which works on providing healthy meals for children affected by poverty and hunger and offers educational programming to combat food insecurity.

It feels good to support local initiatives that bring healthy food options to the community. Even as I write, I believe the world is opening up, growing, and shape-shifting into new patterns. I will put my trust in the people who care and in the people who are working to ensure that these new patterns move us—and all who share this planet—forward, in nourishing and loving ways.

CHAPTER THREE
INDIGENOUS WISDOM

"Pachamama is always healing us with her sacred plant medicine."

— PUMA FREDY QUISPE SINGONA,
ANDEAN MEDICINE MAN

ONE EARTH FAMILY

A patch of blue appears through a thick cloud cover, birds loudly chirp, and the sky gradually grows lighter with the start of a new day.

Sun. Sky. Breath. Life.

I notice the sun's arc is now rising more in the south-east. The early morning light is awe-inspiring once I locate it on the horizon. But it shines only momentarily before clouds once again dim the soft glow. Just like us, I suppose —here shining brightly and then, at least in physical form, gone too soon with scarcely a trace of our presence to be found. Sometimes, though, the luminosity behind the clouds penetrates through the overcast sky like a beacon leading us toward some distant land we cannot yet see.

Similar to the nearby pileated woodpecker pecking loudly against a tree trunk, I am busy working today. A writing project focused on how to protect nature feels daunting—as well as frequently discouraging and often depressing. Nonetheless, there are reasons for hope and for gratitude. As a writer, I am an observer—sometimes a poet and philosopher as well. As a woman, I am a creator, giving birth to art, music, dance, and songs—a sacred vessel no less so than the rivers, waterfalls, and clouds above. All women are creators of this world. We are the rivers, the tides, and the moon. We are Mother Earth.

Meanwhile, our days unfold. We don't know what each new day will offer or what we will bring to it. I try to remain open. Aware. Patient. I walk my path with the support of all I hold close to my heart. I listen. I embrace. I release.

Today, I feel a heavy sadness within.

A hawk lands on the tree branch in the yard. *"Don't give up before you've barely begun,"* it seems to say. I remind myself that I have access to joy as well as to sorrows. I recall the birth of my daughters: deep-brown inquisitive eyes and delicate, tiny fingers. I recall sunrises over ocean waves and a brilliant full moon high in the sky on a clear night. These are the things of hope, not despair. That is the path I choose to follow, with deep truth. And with deep love.

I glimpse at the hawk with wings spread wide as it soars off.

"She Who Walks with the Moon" is who I am from a long-ago naming ceremony. I have Ojibwa/Chippewa ancestral roots from my grandmother's side of our family tree. Little Flower is the name of my great-great-grandmother—small in stature, white hair, from St. Joseph Island, Michigan. She is one branch of a family tree that now contains various branches. Unfortunately, this particular branch has been severed not only from modern society but also from much of my own knowing. Sometimes, I catch a glimpse of this ancestral connection or tune into it in ways I don't discuss. That ancestry is there when I need it. But I am more than one branch of an extensive family tree that contains numerous lineages. I am also on this Earth as a human: a member of our global human family.

Are we not *all* children of this Earth, as well as children of the stars, deeply connected to the land, water, sun, and moon? Are we not all one family on this beautiful planet? Can we honor the branches of our unique heritages while also appreciating that each branch is connected to a greater whole? Can we likewise appreciate that we are part of the Earth's larger family with kinships to animals, birds, fish, and even the smallest living organism in the soil?

Recognizing the interconnected branches and deep roots of our Earth family reminds us that we are inextricably linked to our ecosystems. We are not separate from the living beings who share our home, nor are we independent of Mother Earth. Think of the vast underground system of tree roots in a forest, or even the tree roots in our city parks and neighborhoods. Our connections likewise ground us to one another—and to all living beings—on this amazing planet, going so much deeper than our individual human selves.

Who are we when we take the time to remember? How do we learn to welcome the energetic, divine spark of each living thing? How do we become a caring global Earth family?

I listen within and hear:

"Stop trying to control the movement of the tides. Instead, sink into your own power as a magnificent Earth creature. We are on this glorious planet but for a brief moment in time."

Breathe. Release. Love.

TRUTH TELLING

I received an invitation from a friend to travel to the Native American Educational and Cultural Center in West Lafayette, Indiana, to hear birch bark canoe artist Wayne Valliere and his apprentice, Lawrence Mann, share their knowledge of Anishinaabe traditions and culture in protecting our Earth home. In the presentation, I hear a story of Indians who long ago traveled by canoe to a land where food grew upon the water: wild rice. Today, Wayne says, the wild rice on the Wisconsin reservation faces many threats.

Wild rice requires shallow waters to germinate and does not do well in the Upper Midwest without harsh winters. Consequently, warmer winters and extreme weather events are having a negative effect on the availability of wild rice. Water pollution threats can also pose harms to wild rice. For the Anishinaabe people, these wild plants not only serve as an important food source but are an integral part of their cultural heritage.

After the presentation, I sit in a circle with Wayne and a few others in the group to discuss what our Earth home needs. I am there to listen, respectfully and with an open heart.

Wayne tells me about the cultural genocide of his people by the White man. How the healers—the medicine men—were put into prisons. The American Medical Association (AMA) had decided that it needed control over the people selling elixirs. But the AMA then went after Indian medicine men who had knowledge of healing plants for their tribes. The tribes lost a whole generation of knowledge of the plants and of the Indian ways.

I can *feel* the anger behind his words. The hurt. The determination.

He says to me, "Tell the truth."

I wonder what that means. "Tell the truth." He repeats it again, more firmly this time.

Perhaps before we can talk about healing the Earth, we must acknowledge and heal the injustices toward Native American tribes and toward Indigenous Peoples across the globe. Healing the Earth goes hand-in-hand with honoring the ways of the Indigenous Peoples who live in harmony and in balance with nature.

Wayne tells me that our Earth home is Grandmother Earth because grandmother is the person you go to for help; she has experience and wisdom. He talks about the importance of raising children with an understanding of caring for Grandmother Earth. He explains that the Wisconsin reservation can serve as a model for others.

A person in our circle mentions the hydrogen car commercial with Jack Nicolson back in the 1970s. "We had the technology back then," he says. One of the women in the circle nods affirmatively when I ask if I should also discuss solutions in my book.

The group tells me, "The trees are our brothers and sisters. They are family."

Another person and friend, Nils "Buster" Landin— Anishinaabe and member of the Tlingit Tribe—mentions his anger with Native American museums that act like Indigenous People are a thing of the past, a relic. "We are here, right now, living! We are not gone," he says.

I leave the gathering with a message that isn't necessarily easy to hear: *Recognize the horrific harms the White man has inflicted on the American Indians and on Grandmother Earth, and change your ways.*

PROPHETSTOWN

The following day, I visit Prophetstown State Park, operated by the Indiana Department of Natural Resources.
According to the State Park website, this park is named
after a Native American village established by a great
Shawnee leader, Tecumseh, and his brother, Tenskwatawa
—also known as the Prophet—in 1808.

Tecumseh set up this village when White settlers
forced the tribe to leave their homeland in Ohio. With a
vision of forming a coalition of Native people to control
their own destiny, Tecumseh invited other tribal nations to
join together. Then in 1811, Indiana territorial governor,
William Henry Harrison (later President Harrison), marched an army to the village while Tecumseh was
away. Fearing an attack, the Prophet decided that the best
course of action was to strike first. After the battle, the
governor's troops burned what was left of the village to
the ground.

There isn't much to see at the Prophetstown village
today. The few structures that are displayed do not appear
to be fully representative of the rich heritage of the Native
American people.

The surrounding land does include 900 acres of native
prairie grasses with wetlands, wet slopes called fens,
prairie, and open woodlands. Walking along the trail, I
come upon a dump site where the park discards old equipment and scrap that likely needs repair or has been left
here as garbage. The location of the dump so close to the
village strikes me as incredibly disrespectful. It makes me
sad and reminds me of how vital it is to ensure that
Indigenous People lead the way when doing something "in
their memory." This historic site seems to need a nonprofit
run by Native Americans to tell the story of their past,

their living present, and their future in a way that is truthful and respectful.

Before leaving, I stop by the Prophetstown visitor center, which is small. It has glass aquariums containing turtles and snakes. One turtle pushes up against the glass as though to say, *"Let me out!"* I can't imagine being that poor turtle confined to a glass cage every day. Why not take children outside to observe turtles in a pond instead of teaching them to treat living creatures without the reverence and care they deserve?

I understand why some of the Indigenous People at the Native American Educational and Cultural Center are angry. No one is listening to them. The government wants the credit for saying, "Look, we have a park dedicated to Native American tribes." Yet it doesn't want to own up to the genocides and atrocities enacted against the Native American people, nor does it want to embrace the teachings of Indigenous ways.

Overall, the visit leaves me feeling unsettled.

HEALING OUR PAST

This afternoon, a woman I never met sends me an email invitation to attend a healing fire ceremony carried out in the Lakota tradition. She heard a radio interview I gave a few years ago regarding one of my books on grief and wants me to meet her friend, a Lakota healer.

When I meet the Lakota healer, he tells me that I am like a frightened fox and that I need to release the fears from my past and look toward the future, knowing bear (spirit animal) is there for me to offer strength.

It's true. I had been struggling with personal issues that were causing me to feel fearful. I never know how or why things unfold as they do, but I am grateful that, at times, what we need during our life challenges appears.

As I sit by the fire during the ceremony, I observe the peacefulness of the land surrounding us. It's a lovely spot with mature, old-growth trees. Distant birds caw, the trees sway their branches, and the clouds drift gently by with a quiet whisper: *"All is well."*

Each person here meets with the Lakota healer. So many people are carrying deep wounds—some physical, some emotional, and some spiritual. These stories need to be heard and understood, especially if the cause of the wounding has been overlooked or disregarded in modern culture.

After the healing ceremony and shared meal, I return home and sit for a while in my yard. The squirrels are loudly chattering, and a chipmunk suddenly scurries across the drive, making a mad dash for cover beneath a nearby bush. Another squirrel sits on top of the picnic table, watching a fat cat that is slowly creeping into the yard. I shoo away the cat! Outdoor cats are such a menace to wildlife, including the bird population. I prefer attracting birds, not having them get scared off or eaten by feline predators. Once the cat is safely out of the area, the squirrels continue scavenging for nuts.

A crow cackles.

If we are going to heal the Earth and be able to hear what is needed to do so, we have to ensure that our inner channel is open, not blocked by wounds that we have failed to address, individually or collectively as a society. My personal wounds from long-standing family addiction issues were weighing heavy on me. Perhaps as I open one gate for Spirit, it opens a Spirit gate for others as well. Perhaps as we heal, our Earth home also heals.

Another neighboring cat hides in the foliage, and a squirrel high on a tree branch shakes its tail and chatters in that direction. A warning. Beware.

As we spend time in nature, will we learn to identify

cautionary telltale signs and recognize what we must do? Will Grandmother Earth reveal her wisdom to humans who are willing to open their hearts and listen?

INDIGENOUS ENVIRONMENTAL KNOWLEDGE

This morning, I am speaking with Billie Warren, a Pokagon Potawatomi citizen and founder of Jibek Mbwakawen Inc., an environmental nonprofit working to connect people back to the land from an Indigenous perspective. Interestingly, non-Indigenous people are usually accustomed to introducing themselves by their name and then, when asked, their job title: teacher, nurse, attorney, accountant, and so on. Many Indigenous Peoples introduce themselves by their name—birth name or a sacred name gifted by elders—and then their tribe, their clan, and their vocation—such as: "My name is Billie Warren, a citizen of the Pokagon Band of Potawatomi, of the Bear Clan, a water protector, seed keeper, and steward of the land." In Native American cultures, Billie says, "We belong to a community rather than identifying as an I."

Billie works as an educational and environmental consultant who shares Indigenous history and ecological knowledge at universities, museums, public schools, national parks, nonprofit organizations, and conservation groups. With her university science training and rich Indigenous heritage, she serves as a bridge between Western science and the environmental knowledge of Native people. As she explains, Western science and Indigenous knowledge must work together for a broader perspective. One example she gives is our understanding of the milkweed plant. Western science teaches that the milkweed plant is vital for monarch butterflies. Yet that plant is also historically significant to Native people as medicine.

She explains that Indigenous Peoples are often acknowledged only when referencing their spirituality rather than being recognized for the expertise they hold in numerous fields. She points out, "Our calendar systems, our math systems, and our advances were erased, and we were lied to in our history books." School curriculums, for instance, mention the American Indian fur trade but fail to include the genocide of Native Americans. Billie notes that the Homestead Act of 1862 encouraged White Western migration and distributed millions of acres of tribal ancestral land, displacing Indigenous Peoples from their village homelands. According to the Holocaust Museum Houston:

> When European settlers arrived in the Americas, historians estimate there were over 10 million Native Americans living there. By 1900, their estimated population was under 300,000. Native Americans were subjected to many different forms of violence, all with the intention of destroying the community.

The intentional spread of diseases, the massacres and wars against Native Americans, and the forced removals from their villages were catastrophic. Billie says, "It is one of the largest holocausts in the world."

Billie's work also includes educating groups about the cultural genocide of her people. She points out that a lot of people view Native Americans through a lens of being like the dinosaurs, only existing in the past and not here in the present day. Even today, policies prevent Indigenous Peoples from foraging for the medicines they need, which are not found in urban neighborhoods but rather in government-owned parks. Some of their medicine is only found in wetlands, swamps, and marshes, and those natural areas are being drained and eliminated.

Billie wants non-Indigenous people to understand this cultural genocide from both a historical perspective, where their language and religious practices were declared illegal, and also from today's environmental perspective. She says, "I would love to have clean water and teach people to connect to the land. We are all one, and we are all connected."

One way to bring public awareness of these wrongs is via a Land Acknowledgment Statement recognizing the Indigenous Peoples who were killed and displaced from their homelands. For example, Indiana University in Bloomington has the following statement on its website: "Indiana University wishes to acknowledge and honor the Indigenous communities native to this region, and recognize that Indiana University – Bloomington was built on Indigenous homelands and resources. Indiana University recognizes the Miami, Delaware, Potawatomi, and Shawnee people as past, present, and future caretakers of this land. We are proud to support Native students in their pursuit of community and success at Indiana University."

Such statements are, of course, only a starting point. Across the globe, we are beginning to understand that Indigenous Peoples everywhere need to have their voices heard. The time for listening and for honoring the ways of living in balance is here.

A useful way to begin bridging the gap in knowledge —and to better understand what is needed for healing—is to visit an Indigenous cultural center run by Indigenous Peoples. These Indigenous educational centers can provide a wealth of resources from an Indigenous perspective. We all have much to learn during our life journey here on Grandmother Earth.

LOVE, LIBERATION, AND TRANSFORMATION

During an excellent series of workshops offered by The Shift Network, a global transformation education network, I listen to the teachings of Puma Fredy Quispe Singona, Andean medicine man and shaman. Puma tells us that this sacred journey on Pachamama—our Earth Mother—requires healing ourselves, healing our human family, and connecting to our Cosmic Mother.

Puma explains that it's necessary to heal ourselves first, noting that we can't give to others what we don't have ourselves. He says that we need to transform our negative emotions away from the heavy energies we don't want, such as depression, doubt, anger, guilt, and fear. We can then shift into the lighter energies we wish to embody, such as happiness, joy, peace, and love. As we do so, he says, we will vibrate on a more loving frequency and can be of service to our community.

According to Puma, we should ask not what to do but *how* to do it. Just being love, being peace, and being compassionate is a healing service we can offer to our global family and to our Cosmic Mother. When we embody love and set our intentions to be of service in love, we will no longer operate on the low vibrations of trauma, depression, doubt, guilt, and fear. Instead, we shift out of these old paradigms. We begin new cycles. And we restore our relationship with our Earth Mother.

During the opening and closing ceremonies for our group presentations, Puma reminds us that we are *always* in ceremony. Everything we do should be in service, in love, and in gratitude for our global family. The purpose of prayer and ceremony, he says, is to reach harmony. With harmony, we find inner peace, which is the best medicine in times of chaos.

Love, Puma emphasizes, is liberating and transformational. If we plant seeds of love and joy, we will harvest love and joy. That is an important message for us as we collectively undertake this work of transformation for ourselves, for our families, and for our Earth home. The Noqan Kani Global Community Center in Peru and The Shift Network offer numerous opportunities for learning more about these sacred, ancestral teachings. I highly recommend this life-changing source of wisdom.

Puma concludes his teachings by saying to everyone in attendance: "Infinite blessings and love to you all, my beautiful family."

PART TWO
HOPE

CHAPTER FOUR
HOPE BLOOMS

"There is something infinitely healing in the repeated refrains of nature—the assurance that dawn comes after night, and spring after winter."

— RACHEL CARSON,
BIOLOGIST/AUTHOR

THE WORLD AWAKENS IN SPRING

It's April, and I am visiting my in-laws in Southern Indiana. The forsythias are already in full bloom with bright yellow flowers. A rabbit hops along a row of bushes, and a clear blue sky stretches out over the wide-open landscape. As I sit on a glider in the yard, a red-bellied woodpecker with black and white speckled wings squawks at me as though warding me off from the suet hanging in the bird feeder. A gorgeous woodpecker with a red velvety head and smooth dark-black wings stopped by earlier, along with a brown thrush and a red-winged blackbird. The lilac bush in their yard is beginning to show buds— everything here blooming a few weeks ahead of my home in Central Indiana. Small rhubarb leaves are the only visible vegetation in the garden.

Everything feels so tranquil on this hill overlooking the nearby farmlands. I hear a mockingbird call from high up on a tree branch, and when walking along the lane that leads up from the country road, I can hear spring peepers in the distant wooded wetland areas that serve as windbreaks from storms during inclement weather. Hawks glide over the fields in search of a meal. Usually, I see the hawks high in the sky. Today, however, one hawk swept so fast and low across a nearby field that at first glance, I thought it was a coyote.

Our meals with my husband's family focus more on what is in season than on a grocery store list. Strawberries from the garden in May mean homemade jam on toast for breakfast. Blueberries in June mean fresh fruit for breakfast or a blueberry pie for dessert after dinner. Persimmons in the fall mean pudding, and pecans from neighboring trees across the lane might go into bread or Thanksgiving pies. Green onions, radishes, asparagus, potatoes, tomatoes, zucchini, green beans, and lettuce all come from the garden, where they get harvested when ripe and served for that evening's meal. My father-in-law, Russ, at age ninety-four, is outside throwing compost onto the garden as I write.

Russ and Dorothy, my in-laws, don't forgo all use of refined sugar, but they use it sparingly in recipes that call for it. Locally harvested honey is often their go-to sweetener. They also aren't drinking soda pop or alcohol. They aren't eating store-bought snacks and have rarely eaten at fast-food places. Dorothy recently turned ninety-one, and she is active, happy, and healthy. Observing their lifestyle and longevity, I notice that they walk daily and stay busy with the garden and housework.

Years past, they raised their seven children on produce

from their large vegetable garden, along with apples, pears, peaches, and apricots from their orchard and wild berries from bushes that grew in the field. Back when Dorothy's brother still had a small dairy herd that roamed the fields, their meat consumption and milk supply came directly from the cows. There are no highways with heavy traffic close by and no nearby factories and commercial buildings. As a side note, for people interested in what may possibly be contributing to their longevity, they are also generally both good-natured. Their seven adult children, aged fifty to sixty-eight, are all healthy, and Dorothy and Russ now have a slew of grandchildren and a few great-grandchildren as well.

Early spring here is a showcase of flowering dogwoods, yellow daffodils, and rosy pink blooms. It's marvelous. Without the incessant noise of traffic, sirens, and maintenance crews found when living in a city, you can hear more clearly the variety of bird chatter: rapid peeps, low trills, high whistles, caws, and endless variations of bird calls along with the buzz and fluttering wings of insects.

Fruits and vegetables are not yet ready for picking this early in the season, but the world is definitely awake and vibrating with song. Wildlife critters are likely readying their homes, seeking mates, or basking in the return of warm sunlight as everything readies for new growth.

FERTILE LAND

The following day, I visit the farm owned by Dorothy's brother to speak with his son Pat. It's 48°F with bright sunlight overhead and crisp air. As I head onto their prop-erty, I see a killdeer, which is a distinctive bird with spindly legs and black stripes across its white chest. Having grown up in an urban environment, I am always thrilled to discover creatures that are new to me.

The land managed by Pat looks incredibly green compared to the dry brown ground of neighboring farms. As I walk up the drive, I notice that one of the buildings on the property has rooftop solar panels.

I meet Pat in the Honey House where pipes from the hot water heater warm the floor. He is busy putting lids on jars of honey; PJB Honey is one of the family's business ventures. Pat remarks on the loss of honey bee populations, due in part because there is less clover and fewer native wildflowers. Most farmers spray generous amounts of pesticides and herbicides and also plant a non-native grass known as fescue, which has taken over the land that used to have beneficial pollinator-friendly ground cover such as clover, buckwheat, and bird's-foot trefoil.

But I'm not here to talk about bees. I know we need pollinator plants. I know we are in serious trouble without the bees. I am meeting with Pat today to learn about his regenerative farming practices.

Pat notes that chemical poisons are everywhere in the farming community. As mentioned in the Preface, he states that the overuse and dependence on chemicals arose after World War II when the big chemical plants had all these chemicals that were no longer needed. So, Pat says, they found that nitrogen, for example, that had been used for making bombs would also make plants grow and green up. Chemicals began to be widely used as herbicides and pesticides—potent poisons—and companies made a lot of money renaming these chemicals, formerly used during warfare, and then marketing and selling the chemicals to farmers. As he says, "We thought we were smarter than nature. Big agricultural industries and universities bought into the use of chemicals as fertilizers, herbicides, pesticides, and fungicides, and that generated a lot of money.

Meanwhile, we became addicted to the chemicals, despite the dead zones these poisons create." He points out that these poisons absolutely have a negative effect on the foods we eat, with a direct correlation between tillage, chemical use, and human diseases related to the lack of nutrition and the residual chemicals on the food we consume.

Both humans and plants need nutrients for good health. Pat explains that plants draw minerals, which are essential plant nutrients, from the soil through their roots and nutrients from the air through their leaves. The use of pesticides and herbicides weakens soil health because it reduces the soil's micro-organisms. Like humans, a stronger plant immune system can fight off diseases. With their weakened immune systems, the plants can't fight off pests and diseases. So, the farmers use more pesticides, exacerbating the cycle. In underscoring the critical role of soil health, Pat says that the Food and Agriculture Organization found, "One teaspoon of soil contains more living organisms than there are people in the world."

Regrettably, much of the food we consume today no longer contains the nutrients it did generations ago. Tomatoes grown year-round, for instance, may look pretty. But because they are shipped across the world, they are picked while still green. Pat says vegetables and fruits get a lot of their nutrients right before they ripen. As a result, we cut short the nutritional processes of the plant and, therefore, don't get the full nutrients when we eat them. According to Pat, regenerative farming brings health back to the soil and, thereby, results in more nutrient density in our food.

While recounting regenerative agriculture principles, Pat refers me to a book, *Dirt to Soil* by Gabe Brown, a farmer who lives on a ranch in North Dakota. Concerning the principles of soil health, Pat says farmers and ranchers need to follow five of the following six practices, at minimum, in order to regenerate the soil, with only step six—

livestock integration—not being required, though animal integration would be helpful as well according to Gabe:

1. Context. An understanding of how distinct temperatures and various types of land will result in different plant needs.
2. Limit disturbance. In other words, no tillage.
3. Armor the soil. Use native cover crops for soil protection.
4. Diversity. A multitude of native plants helps regenerate the soil and keeps a variety of microbes living in the soil.
5. Living roots. Keep plant roots in the soil year-round.
6. Animal integration. Allow animals to forage and use manure to increase the soil's organic matter.

Gabe discusses in his book how he learned, through personal farming failures, the need to adopt new habits when it comes to regenerative farming. He emphasizes that we have to look at the whole ecosystem and adopt holistic principles for healthy soil. The practices for soil health provide habitat for pollinators, predator insects, earthworms, and all the microbiology that drives ecosystem function. Native plant roots in the soil also assist with water retention and improve the quality of the water. He further notes that these regenerative farming practices, such as livestock integration, result in carbon sequestration (i.e., absorbing carbon into the soil to help reduce global warming).

Gabe's overall message is extremely valuable: "Without healthy soil, we cannot have healthy crops, healthy animals, or healthy people. We must promote the health and function of the ecosystems in which we farm.

Like humans, nature can handle occasional stress. But just like humans, nature cannot function properly in the face of prolonged or acute stress."

When I look at Pat's lush green farm landscape—while listening to the birds and observing the wildlife—I believe such regenerative soil practices benefit not only humans but all life on our beautiful Earth home.

ANIMAL FACTORY FARMS

As Gabe points out in his book, *Dirt to Soil*, animals have grazed the land for eons, serving an important part of the diverse biosystem needed for healthy land. (See the "Prairie Restoration" section where The Nature Conservancy reintroduced bison to the land to support biodiversity.) Just to be clear, Gabe's regenerative farming practices include livestock but are not at all like large-scale cattle factory farms. That is the exact opposite of what he advocates, which is animal integration and animal foraging on his family farm. Factory farms, also known as concentrated animal feeding operations, or CAFOs, are where large numbers of animals are kept in extreme confinement, often spending their entire lives inside.

People working to mitigate climate change take issue with large-scale cattle livestock, finding the beef industry to be especially damaging to our environment. According to the World Resources Institute, "The world needs to reduce emissions from fossil fuels *and* agriculture to sufficiently rein in global warming." Beef production, through agricultural processes and land-use changes, causes the emission of methane, a potent greenhouse gas. Per the World Resources Institute, "Beef is one of the world's most resource- and emissions-intensive foods, with land use and greenhouse gas emissions 7 times higher than chicken and 20 times higher than beans per gram of protein."

In preindustrial times, we didn't have the automobiles, airplanes, factories, and other fossil fuel emissions like we do now. Moreover, the United States didn't have the high levels of beef consumption coming primarily from large factory farms, so perhaps the potent greenhouse gas produced by cattle wasn't an issue historically. Numerous sources indicate that it is a significant problem today in addressing climate change.

Another criticism related to large-scale beef production is that we should produce more food varieties on our lands rather than our current monocultural agricultural practices: boost our productivity rather than growing so much grain and corn just to feed livestock! The Irish potato famine is a prime example of the potential harms from monoculture in our food supply. Moving away from monoculture farming of one item—such as corn used to feed livestock and to produce high fructose corn syrup—and instead diversifying our locally produced fruits and vegetables means we save on fossil fuels currently used to ship these foods long distances. Locally available food varieties also ensure food security when other countries experience problems with their food supply chain due to wars or climate disruptions.

Finally, a strong case against the beef industry is that we should protect our precious natural ecosystems by preserving forests, prairies, wetlands, and woody savannas: an approach that encourages using the land wisely and sparingly. As noted in "A Love of Trees" chapter, forests across the globe are being destroyed to make space for cattle grazing and cattle feed. Restoring and preserving our natural ecosystems in turn helps mitigate climate change.

One major way we can aid the planet is by reducing

our meat consumption, beef in particular. Reducing beef consumption to even once a week is a helpful place to begin. If you are a meat eater, try doing something like Meatless Mondays, a campaign with plant-based recipes and resources. You might also consider replacing beef with beans or chicken. If you do purchase meat, and can afford to do so, try to ensure the animals are local, forage-raised with nongenetically modified organisms (non-GMO feed).

As we gain access to more locally grown healthy food options, such choices will hopefully become more afford-able for everyone. Health experts tell us that eating vegeta-bles and salads is good for our health. Too much red meat —and processed meats such as hot dogs, sausage, lunch meat, and bacon—may put us at higher risk of heart diseases, strokes, and diabetes. Of course, the vegetables we consume should come from soil that is healthy, containing beneficial microorganisms and without chem-ical poisons.

EARTH DAY

After visiting Pat's farm, I return home. Spring in the Midwest means the trees are full of blossoms, the ground is a showcase of dandelions and small white spring beau-ties, and the bluebells are spreading their sleepy leaves upward, though not yet flowering. A pair of bluebirds survey my yard, maybe deciding if this is a place to call home or if it is just a stopover as they travel elsewhere.

It is unseasonably hot today. Every few days, the weather changes from a light snow covering to a heat spell that feels like summer and then back again.

My husband and I are attending an Earth Day event near our neighborhood. It's hosted by a nearby commu-nity association, in the front parking lot, with food trucks and vendor booths. While there, I stop by the Elders Climate Action booth. This group's mission is to mobilize older individuals across the United States to address climate change while there is still time to protect the well-being of our grandchildren and future generations of children. They offer a wealth of information about ways to get involved. I also gather useful educational materials from other environmental organizations, such as Keep Indianapolis Beautiful and Citizens Climate Lobby, and I briefly stop by an electric car display.

While there is an abundance of family-friendly nature-based programming, my husband notices a State Farm Insurance table where representatives are passing out invasive bamboo plants to children. A lot of children are walking around with this invasive plant! My husband talks to the staff members at this booth, who seem to be unaware of the problem but agree to tell the children to keep the bamboo plants indoors. It's already late in the day, and I wonder how many of those invasive plants will end up in the soil. Other booths have additional problems: nonrecyclable plastic cups and plastic trinkets.

When I learn of another upcoming Earth Day event at a nearby park, I email the event organizer regarding the invasive bamboo plant issue. Despite my email, State Farm is again at a display table passing out bamboo plants. The plants are not in soil, so their argument may be that the bamboo plant is merely decorative. In hindsight, I should have emailed State Farm directly about my concerns, because people walking around with a highly invasive plant at an Earth Day event makes no sense. The unnecessary paper handouts, plastics, and garbage at large public gatherings can also be discouraging, though there is much less of that here than at many outdoor events.

I am not trying to criticize Earth Day celebrations or the numerous organizations working on sustainability and eco-friendly green initiatives. On the contrary, these efforts are commendable. For instance, although the State Farm representatives were passing out bamboo plants, the company website indicates a commitment to sustainability with an Environmental Sustainability Team, LEED-certified buildings—which means leadership in energy and environmental building design—and an elimination of all single-use plastic bottles. That is definitely great news!

But if we are participating in a lack of awareness regarding invasive plant species or in unmindful plastic pollution at an Earth Day celebration, imagine what businesses, organizations, families, and individuals are doing on a large scale—and on a daily basis—that is contributing to our environmental problems.

My point is that we can *all* do better toward our Earth care efforts when planning work conferences, entertainment/performance events, wedding gatherings, religious celebrations, dining services, educational symposiums, sporting activities, and so on. Some solutions are not that complicated: eliminate single-use plastics, sell or encourage the use of reusable beverage containers, use QR Codes, carry cloth bags for shopping, and utilize native plants if landscaping is involved. To be clear, I have made mistakes myself. A few decades back, I planted a vine under the trees in my yard that turned out to be invasive! A willingness to learn and to change is the goal.

Hopefully, as we grow in our understanding about caring for our Earth home, we will make better choices. As poet Maya Angelou said, "Do the best you can until you know better. Then, when you know better, do better." Businesses, organizations, governments, and individuals can implement healthier Earth-friendly choices by periodically assessing the environmental effects of their actions and figuring out how to make improvements where feasible. For instance, we can get rid of plastic water bottles, plastic straws, and plastic cutlery, and stop distributing plastic trinkets that just ends up in a landfill somewhere.

Before leaving the Earth Day event, I have the good fortune to meet the owners of Pure Eating Way, a minority- and woman-owned local food truck offering vegan food options. While there, they explain to me the importance of eating whole plant-based foods, without added chemicals, colors, and artificial flavoring, as well as the benefits of avoiding highly processed foods for our physical health! I enjoy a delicious vegan meal from them. Not insignificantly, they serve their food items in recyclable containers! I make a personal pledge to do better myself in actively choosing which businesses I support.

GETTING RID OF GRASS LAWNS

I am wearing shorts today, though it seems early in the season for such high temperatures. I went on a walk at 10:00 a.m. and felt hot before I had finished my stroll around the neighborhood. It's interesting to observe the neighboring lawns I pass by along my walk: some are entirely green, manicured, and likely sprayed with chemical poisons; and some yards are beautiful with purple violets and yellow dandelions that feed the bees and native pollinators and add vibrant colors to the landscape. I remember my friend in high school telling me that her mom made salads with dandelion leaves.

Of course, the people who spray poisons don't just kill weeds. There are microorganisms on the plants and in the soil, along with the numerous tiny creatures that feed on those miniscule organisms and ingest the poisons. Insecticides sprayed to kill lawn grubs also effectively kill all larvae, including fireflies (known as lightning bugs by some). There is nothing natural or attractive about a green lawn that doesn't offer anything to the creatures who share our landscape and, in some cases, harm the pollinators that we rely on for our food sources. We should be thanking these creatures and offering them more native plants, not working so hard to make our lawns artificially sterile.

Believing a manicured grass yard looks nice is a result of conditioning from advertisements that businesses use to sell chemicals, ideas probably brought to the United States from England with the notion that green lawns equate wealth. People with more disposable income have the money to spend on chemical fertilizers, pesticides, landscape crews, and mowing services. To me, a bland monoculture grass yard is ugly. How absurd we are. Better to have a yard with native flowers, raised beds for vegetable gardens, and tall shade trees. The beauty in the spring colors—light pinks, bright yellows, and shades of purple—are such a gift! Only humans would think to destroy something as lovely as violets.

While on my walk, I listen to the robins, cardinals, and woodpeckers. There's a quote by Mahatma Gandhi, "What you do may seem insignificant to you, but it is most important that you do it." Just getting rid of non-native grass lawns is an enormous step in the right direction!

A SANCTUARY FOR ALL LIVING BEINGS

It is early May, and I am not yet planting my herbs and tomatoes, but soon—usually sometime after Mother's Day —I will begin working in the garden. The sun is out today, and the morning air is cool. It is pleasant.

Everything looks so vibrant this morning after a rainfall last night: the bluebells are now tall rather than droopy, the foliage is lush, and the redbuds are filled with rosy blossoms, a sure sign of spring. What started years ago as a small lilac twig brought home from my mother-in-law's yard is now in full bloom with an exquisite scent that reminds me of my grandmother, who loved lilacs. All these blossoming buds and brightly colored flowers must seem like paradise to the insects and birds. Bees are busy looking for potential homes, and a local farmers' market will open this Saturday.

I watch tiny yellowish catkins (the male flowers) drifting down from the oak tree like soft rain. The pine trees and the evergreen bushes have new lime-green growth on their needles, and I saw my first hummingbird of the season yesterday. A high of 88°F is expected today, and it has already reached 90°F in places like Missouri. I take my walks earlier in the morning because it can get hot quickly and stay hot well into the evening.

In spring, our yard is a beautiful wildlife haven, created with our ongoing care. We have a redbud tree in bloom that we found as a seedling in our flowerbed, likely from one of the seeds dropped by the birds. We planted the seedling near the oaks where it has space to grow and can serve as an understory tree for the much larger mature oaks. I observe a chipmunk playing near the woodpile, darting in and out. A red squirrel (also known as a pine squirrel) makes its way from a pin oak tree near the shed to the picnic table and then hurries to the woodpile near the raspberry and blackberry vines. Meanwhile, a bumble bee buries itself under the dried leaves at the edge of the birdfeeders. Distant dark clouds indicate a storm is approaching. Maybe that is why the bee is going for cover.

So much color and bird activity in one small yard. Drinking my morning coffee while listening to birdsong is a joy. Our yard serves as a sanctuary for butterflies, birds, and numerous other critters. The plants, trees, and brush pile give the squirrels and chipmunks a way to travel safely. If they are forced to cross barren grass, they become exposed to predators such as hawks and cats. As I previ-

ously mentioned, allowing beloved pet cats outdoors decimates the bird population and other small mammals. To
protect birds, indoor cats are a preferable option. (Visit the
National Audubon Society website to read more on that
topic.)

What began as hard clay in our yard is now pliable,
healthy soil. The moles do a skillful job of tunneling,
which mixes soil nutrients, improves aeration of the soil,
and makes it easier for seeds to take root. Those seeds
then become native plants with deep roots that allow the
rainwater to more easily percolate into the soil. As the
plants flower, they provide nourishment for bees, butterflies, dragonflies, hummingbirds, lightning bugs, and
moths. It's all connected.

Just imagine the numerous lifeforms living below the
soil now that it's no longer dry clay! Worms, cicada and
lightning bug larvae, ants, moles, beetles, and other living
organisms thrive in this nourishing community, each
contributing toward a healthy ecosystem. A study
mentioned in *Scientific American*, a scholarly magazine,
found that more than half the world's species live underground! It might be a fun exercise to ask young children
how many creatures they can name that live in the dirt.

SAVING BABY BIRDS

This afternoon, I am meeting with Ellen Jacquart,
program leader for the Indiana Native Plant Society and
former ecologist for The Nature Conservancy. She tells me
that we need native plants. For one thing, native plants
bring the insects that baby birds require as their food
source. Most baby birds are unable to feed on seeds, and
without insects, baby birds can starve to death. As Ellen
says, native plants have a symbiotic relationship with
native wildlife, and those insects support the continuation

and survival of the bird population. Ellen points out that insects are the canary in the coal mine, and their absence demonstrates when the system is disrupted. Everything falls apart if native plants are gone.

What are native plants?

According to the National Wildlife Federation, native plants have evolved or adapted for thousands of years to native wildlife in a particular region and are vital in forming sustainable habitats and ecosystems (as opposed to exotic plants from other parts of the world or plants cultivated by humans into forms that don't exist in nature and do not support wildlife or beneficial native insects). It's important to understand that native plants thrive in the soil and weather conditions of their local region. As mentioned in the "Fertile Land" section, native plants have fewer pest problems and have deep roots that manage rainwater runoff. Consequently, they do not require toxic pesticides and excessive supplemental watering.

As previously noted, insecticides are extremely harmful for pollinators. Ellen explains that neonicotinoids —or neonics for short—are systemic insecticides used to treat crop seeds and ornamental landscaping plants, and these neonics have been strongly implicated in the devastating collapse of pollinator populations around the world. About 70 percent of the world's plants require a pollinator. She says, "Neonics are used as a seed coating in virtually all corn and 75 percent of soybeans planted in the Midwest areas of the United States." A small amount of the seed coating is taken up by the developing corn or soybean plant, and it protects the plant from insect damage; the rest of the seed coating ends up on the soil, moved by the wind, or moved in the water. As she states, a typical application rate of 1.25 milligrams per corn kernel is enough to kill over 150,000 honey bees if it is applied evenly. However, over 90 percent of neonic dust on the seed is not taken up by the growing plant but instead blows away, depositing on soil and water and being taken up by plants growing in the area.

Ellen notes that neonics are also commonly used to treat garden plants, meaning that our gardens may have toxic plants that will kill the very pollinators we are hoping to help. "Literally, a death trap for bees and butterflies," she says emphatically.

What can we do?

On the Indiana Native Plant Society website, Ellen lists the following suggestions:

- Before you buy any seed or plants for your garden, ask whether these items have been treated with neonics. If the answer is yes or they don't know, let them know you won't buy neonic-treated seeds or plants and walk away.
- If you live near farm fields, there is a strong likelihood that neonic-treated crop seed is being used and that it may be in your soil and be taken up by plants in your garden. Ask questions and find out.
- And finally, don't be bothered by insect damage on your garden plants. That is a badge of pride, showing that you have a healthy garden benefiting pollinators.

Ellen is also actively involved with eradicating invasive species. One example of a harmful invasive in several states is the Callery pear tree—native to China and Vietnam and known for its cultivated variety the Bradford pear tree—which has been planted throughout the United States. These trees aggressively invade open areas and forests, displacing native plants. She says that birds need

75 percent of the local plant base to be native so that enough insect larvae are produced to feed the birds' offspring. Callery pear trees choke out native plants, endangering the baby birds' food source.

She mentions that Weed Wrangle is a nationwide undertaking that connects volunteers and public lands in an effort to eradicate non-native invasive plant species and restore native plant communities. As Ellen says, "We need native trees, we need native plants, and we need to reduce invasives."

PRAIRIE RESTORATION

In talking to Ellen, it quickly becomes clear that prairies are a habitat for which she likewise feels great passion. Prairies are ecosystems consisting of native grasses, native wildflowers, and very few trees. They include unique wildlife species that can only live in a prairie, or that thrive best in a prairie habitat, such as black-tailed prairie dogs, American bison, pronghorn antelopes, black-footed ferrets, greater prairie chicken, ornate box turtles, and dozens of grassland birds.

Additionally, grasslands with native plants are a nature-based solution for climate change. Prairie plants have deep roots that sequester carbon into the ground, meaning the plants pull excess carbon out of the atmosphere and store it underground, also referred to as creating a carbon sink.

According to the Nature Conservancy of Canada, prairies are one of the world's most endangered ecosystems. The World Wildlife Fund website likewise contains reports detailing the immense prairie grassland loss across the United States, Canadian, and Mexican portions of the Great Plains. In the Northern Great Plains region, the plowing up of grasslands to plant wheat crops drove the largest loss of native grasslands.

Ellen references her prior work helping with the restoration of Kankakee Sands in Northwest Indiana. Kankakee Sands is 8,400 acres of prairies and wetlands owned by The Nature Conservancy. It serves as a connecting piece between other preserves, totaling over 20,000 acres of natural areas. It consists of more than 600 species of native plants and is home to more than eighty-six rare, threatened, and endangered species, including seventy species of butterflies, along with dragonflies, bees, frogs, lizards, and snakes.

Bison also now roam the Kankakee Sands area. As noted by The Nature Conservancy, bison support the prairies by providing shallow depressions that fill with rain-water and create habitat for amphibians, reptiles, insects, and other plants. As of this writing, there are more than ninety bison at Kankakee Sands grazing on 1,100 acres of the prairie. This restored area, which had been drained for agricultural purposes, was once part of the Grand Kankakee Marsh system—an area of around 500,000 acres, historically referred to as the Everglades of the North.

Ellen explains that we need our prairies, not only for the various rare and endangered species that depend on this habitat for their survival but also because the deep-rooted native prairie plants absorb nutrient pollution—which helps with water quality—and serve as natural carbon sinks that fight climate change by removing CO_2 emitted into the atmosphere by humans.

PRESERVING OUR WETLANDS

The next day, my husband and I plan a nature hike at Beanblossom Bottoms Nature Preserve, a wetland preserve that provides a home for the endangered Indiana bat as well as many other threatened and protected species. Before our hike, I meet with Kate Hammel from Sycamore Land Trust. This nonprofit conservation organization has protected and restored, to date, 11,000 acres of land, including Beanblossom Bottoms Nature Preserve.

With unmistakable sadness, Kate notes that Indiana has lost 85 percent of its wetlands. Wetlands keep the water and soil clean, reduce flooding, recharge groundwater, and help combat climate change. Per Sycamore Land Trust, "Ecosystems with high biodiversity such as wetlands are more stable, adaptable to increasing storms, and likely to survive changes in species makeup as populations change due to higher temperatures and drought." Unfortunately, a majority of Indiana legislators continue to pass laws that make draining wetlands easier for the builders of commercial facilities and housing developments. Such a tremendous and unnecessary loss! We can coexist with nature rather than destroying it. Sycamore Land Trust has 80 acres of wetland restoration, 26,000 native tree plantings, and 7,000 native plants grown from local seed for habitat restoration. A worthy accomplishment indeed!

Sycamore Land Trust also offers outdoor environmental education programs, such as hands-on activities for schoolchildren and public hikes for people of all ages. Kate describes the organization's Wildlife Camera Project with motion-activated cameras that provide a window into the animal kingdom, recording young bobcats, coyote pups, and even a beaver building and repairing its lodge. "The beaver was building a dam that would naturally create a wetland," she says with excitement. "Sycamore Land Trust is giving nature a chance to heal itself!"

After visiting with Kate, my husband and I head over to Beanblossom Bottoms for our hike. A newly constructed boardwalk allows for an enjoyable stroll through the marshy area. It's a marvelous example of a wetland nature preserve serving as a sanctuary for a variety of wildlife. Along our hike, I see frogs, an assortment of birds, and a black snake sunning itself on the boardwalk. With all the marshy water, I was curious if there would be a lot of mosquitoes here later this summer. My husband, a biologist, explains that in a healthy ecosystem, not as many mosquitoes are present because the vast number of birds, bats, frogs, and predatory insects, like dragonflies, keep things in balance more than in grass-dominated yards that don't leave any habitat for turtles, frogs, and snakes.

At a bridge along the boardwalk, I watch a family of geese with their young swim through the dark waters while eating duckweed. Another goose family joins them in the center of the stream—not unlike humans, I suppose, who gather at parks to meet up with friends or relatives for a picnic, celebration, or reunion. Meanwhile, in the distance, a loud goose honks incessantly, perhaps an adolescent pumped with hormones, like teenage male humans who vie for mates or defend their territories by making a ruckus.

Native wildflowers—with purple, pink, white, and yellow blossoms—poke through the green vegetation. With his biology background, my husband knows the plant names: Jack-in-the-pulpit, cutleaf toothwort, mayapple, spring beauty, Dutchman's breeches, trout lily, bloodroot, trillium, fleabane, and others. He enjoys pointing out trees as well: shagbark hickory, Ohio buckeye, sycamore, red and silver maples, and various oak species. When my daughters were young, they also gave names to the wildflowers we saw on our hikes, but not the same as the names my husband calls off. My daughters created whole imaginary worlds within the woods with fairy houses made of tree stumps and colorful flower petals that served as fairy food. Native Americans, too, had their names for the plants and the places I now walk. Naming the things that matter to us is a practice as old as language itself.

On our walk, I see green herons, dragonflies, wasps, and crawdads (known as crayfish in some locales). We spot a large eagle's nest, made of tree limbs and sticks, high up in the tree top. The once federally endangered American bald eagle, along with the state endangered river otter and bobcat, have made a comeback in this area—though they are still listed as protected species.

As we stroll along the boardwalk into a wooded area, the temperature suddenly drops, and I feel a cool breeze. Then as we head back out into the sun, the temperature rises. It's amazing how you can feel the temperature shift, even in a short distance, when walking to and from a shaded tree area.

Sitting on a trail bench near the creek, I pause to look around. I feel a slight breeze and silently ask what the wind might teach us. I see the water below moving through the creek bed; I watch the tree branches sway as they release seeds. I nod in appreciation for this lesson. It's not the wind or the water or the land alone that teaches us. It is understanding how it's all connected. The wind blows across the water's surface, the seeds fly with the wind, the soil where those seeds land is fed by the water and warmed by the sun, and the soil holds the seeds until they grow. Everything is connected to everything else— and all are part of one living, breathing, beautiful planet.

I hear a catbird: calling and calling. *"Pay attention,"* it cries.

On our way out of the nature preserve, we cross paths with three older women wearing wide-brimmed hats and knee-high water boots as they tread through ankle-deep water on a dirt path off the boardwalk trail. They came prepared. We are not. But we make it through the water puddle, with soggy shoes and socks that will dry soon enough. One woman has a pair of binoculars hanging around her neck. With great enthusiasm, she tells me that they sighted forty-one bird species! The women keep a list of bird sightings on a small notepad. Not a bad way to enjoy the day: trekking out to a wetland to bird-watch.

Walking in nature, besides being good exercise, helps clear the mind, creating an inner stillness and a mindful alertness to outer movements, not unlike the acute senses of the creatures who call this wetland their home. The snake sunning itself on the boardwalk earlier, for example, quickly slipped away and frogs in the water along the boardwalk leapt into hiding spaces as our footstep vibrations reached them well ahead of our physical bodies.

This protected marshy wetland is their home. We are merely guests.

MOTHER'S DAY

Back home, I watch an online presentation by The Nature Conservancy about the critical role of wetlands in preventing flooding and enhancing water quality. More drainage of wetlands means more agricultural runoff. In Indiana, we've already had massive losses from drained wetlands. What's more, we have polluted waterways and deaths from various pollution-related diseases. Are any of our state elected officials watching this presentation? Do they care? Or are business profits more important than our water quality and our health? Can we protect what remains of our wetlands? Will people speak up? Will we look to nature-based solutions for solving our problems or just continue to create new problems for humankind?

This week, it has been 90°F. It's so hot for early May! I feel afraid that we're too late on climate change. Depressed, I try to find gratitude and not to get too far ahead of an unknown future. I didn't sleep well. It was hot having the windows open, but I didn't want to turn on the air conditioner the second week of May.

I decide to spend my Mother's Day walking in one of the state parks, appreciating the wonders of our natural areas provided so freely by Mother Earth: fruit trees, nuts, wild berries, medicinal herbs, mushrooms, honey from honeybees, water to drink, and an evening sunset that casts an exquisite red glow across the sky. I tell myself it will be okay.

My affirmation: "Trust that we will be shown what is needed. Trust that we will change course and rally together to prevent further harm to this glorious planet that we love so much."

CHAPTER FIVE

SUMMER HEAT WAVES

"What you do makes a difference, and you have to decide what kind of difference you want to make."

— JANE GOODALL, CONSERVATIONIST

IT'S HOT OUTSIDE!

In summer, the blackberries ripen, dragonflies dart through the air, lightning bugs glimmer while dancing in the night, and outdoor concerts take place across the city and in neighborhood parks. It has been extremely hot outside, 100°F or higher in the Midwest, with excessive heat warnings in various locations around the globe. With such stifling temperatures, it's not enjoyable being outside for too long. The ground is cracked and baked dry, and the branches on the trees are drooping, a few even dropping yellow leaves—no doubt in distress. If this dryness continues, some places will need to implement water restrictions, another reason *not* to have non-native grass lawns anywhere!

Yesterday, I watched ants going in and out of a dust

pile in our backyard. A few of the ants were carrying a dead, dried worm. If the trees and plants are suffering, what's happening below the ground that we can't see? Birds and other wildlife are also in peril during droughts and heat waves. If nature dies off, numerous species die off as well. Climate change puts our water supplies, our food supplies, and our very survival at risk. My friend's relative recently had a stroke after being out in the heat. We are no different than other life forms when it comes to the deadly harms of heat waves and droughts. What is more, increasing temperatures from climate change result in more large-scale wildfires and dust storms, further exacerbating our environmental problems.

Where I live, we had downpours this spring, but the rain was followed by periods of intense hot spells, sometimes with a twenty-degree temperature swing in a matter of days. (As mentioned earlier, we have rain but at the wrong times.) It's so hot that my husband and I don't go outdoors much now. The heat likely affects businesses as well when people decide not to frequent restaurants, shopping plazas, and outdoor venues because it's too hot. When I do go outside, I have to be careful because it's definitely easier to get sunburned in a matter of twenty minutes, rather than getting burned after being out in the sun all day. In other locations across the planet, climate disruptions are far worse than here. But no one is immune.

Of course, industry leaders, government representatives, and individuals can take actions to ensure that our planet—and all the inhabitants of this Earth—thrive. Before getting into some of those solutions, it helps to understand the cause of the crisis; then, we can better figure out what needs to be done. As such, this chapter might initially feel a bit heavy.

Take breaks as needed. Practice self-care and community care. Get together with friends to process. After we understand the root cause of our climate problems, let's brainstorm how we can tackle the serious environmental challenges facing us. (See more in the "Forming Earth Sustainability Circles" chapter.)

HAZARDS OF FOSSIL FUELS

The United Nations states that, by far, the largest contributor to global climate change is caused by the burning of fossil fuels: **coal, oil, and natural gas**. That's why getting away from our dependence on these resources is absolutely critical! As Katharine Hayhoe pointedly says in her book, *Saving Us*:

> According to the *Carbon Majors Report* produced by the Colorado-based Climate Accountability Institute, one hundred fossil fuel companies have been responsible for emitting 70 percent of the world's heat-trapping gases since 1988. . . . They've gotten rich at the expense of everyone who's being impacted by climate change—and at least some of them want to keep it that way.

The U.S. Environmental Protection Agency (EPA) indicates that there are over 3,400 fossil fuel–fired power plants in the United States. Besides contributing to global climate change, burning fossil fuels create pollutants "known to contribute to adverse health outcomes, including the development of heart or lung diseases, such as asthma and bronchitis, increased susceptibility to respiratory and cardiac symptoms, greater numbers of emergency room visits and hospital admissions, and premature deaths."

While China and India are the biggest users of coal-powered plants, the United States is right behind with many states still utilizing coal for the bulk of their energy. Per the Environmental Integrity Project:

> About 400 coal-fired power plants across the U.S. account for about a third of the nation's carbon dioxide emissions from fossil fuels, as well as releases into the air of soot-like particles, mercury, sulfur dioxide, and nitrogen oxides that cause heart and asthma attacks, pollute waterways, and contaminate fish. These same coal-fired power plants also pipe millions of pounds of arsenic, lead, mercury, and other toxins directly into our rivers and streams. In fact, the EPA has determined that coal-fired generators are the largest industrial source of toxic water discharges in the U.S. today.

At the time of this writing, Indiana tops the list in the United States with more coal-fired power plants than any other state! By way of contrast, Portugal has closed all its coal plants, as have other European countries such as Belgium, Austria, and Sweden.

As noted, coal ash poses significant health hazards as well. A report by the Environmental Integrity group and Earthjustice found that in the states that burn coal, "Coal ash—the toxic waste left after burning coal for electricity —is one of the largest industrial waste streams in the United States. . . . 91% of U.S. coal plants are causing unsafe levels of groundwater contamination. Most coal plants are contaminating groundwater with unsafe levels of arsenic, which is known to cause multiple types of cancer and to impair the brains of developing children." The report adds, "Unsafe levels of toxic metals in ground-water at coal plants threaten the safety of the nation's drinking water as well as the health and safety of lakes and rivers near the plants."

A recent article in *Inside Climate News*, an independent

and nonpartisan news organization, indicates that in Montana, "Republican lawmakers have passed legislation that bars state agencies from considering climate change when permitting large projects that require environmental reviews, including coal mines and power plants." Consequently, a group of youth in Montana sued the state government for its pro-fossil fuel energy policies as a violation of their rights to a "clean and healthful environment." (See more in the "Environmental Lawsuits" section.)

People suffer irreparable harm when industry leaders and elected officials do not adequately safeguard the public health. Granted, there are federal and state government representatives who are working diligently for our welfare and for the health of our planet. But if they are not doing so, then—like the youth in Montana—we need to demand our right to a healthy environment.

DROUGHTS AND WILDFIRES

Burning fossil fuels not only generates toxic emissions that drive climate change, but it also causes a domino effect that results in added environmental problems. The National Institute of Environmental Health Sciences states, "Vehicle emissions, fuel oils and natural gas to heat homes, byproducts of manufacturing and power generation, particularly coal-fueled power plants and fumes from chemical production, are the primary sources of human-made air pollution." Climate change and air pollution are connected. For instance, climate change results in drier soil and drier vegetation. Such drought conditions create more intense wildfire seasons. More intense wildfires cause more air pollution.

As we have witnessed, wildfires—such as those in Canada, Hawaii, Greece, California, Australia, and elsewhere across the planet—release harmful smoke that can increase air pollution to unsafe levels, even in distant areas. When the skies in New York City turned eerily orange and air quality levels reached hazardous levels due to extensive wildfires in Canada, the term "ecocide" was used by young people and adults viewing this unprecedented environmental apocalypse. Ecocide simply means large-scale and systemic destruction of our environment caused by humans.

Similarly with the horrific fires in Maui, the term apocalypse was an apt description for the destruction in Lahaina, an area referred to as sacred land of the heart chakra. Interestingly, an article in *Smithsonian Magazine* notes that non-native invasive grasses in Maui, which are highly flammable, "had transformed the island into a giant tinderbox." These grasses were introduced to Hawaii by Europeans as livestock forage. The invasive non-native grasses, along with Hawaii's drought conditions and hurricane winds, fueled the deadly wildfires that decimated Lahaina.

Clearly, Mother Earth is sending an urgent message, for those who are listening.

EXTREME AIR POLLUTION

According to the Environmental Protection Agency, sensitive groups are especially at risk from air pollution, including children, older adults, and people with health issues such as diabetes, heart disease, or lung disease. Pregnant women are also at risk. Of course, poor air quality doesn't just affect humans, it can also cause harm to animals, plants, and birds. Our beloved pets are vulnerable as well. When air quality reaches hazardous levels, everyone's health is threatened.

In the United States, sites such as AirNow report daily

air quality information for each state using the Air Quality Index (AQI). High index numbers put human health in peril from air pollution, including risks of lung cancer, asthma, and chronic obstructive pulmonary disease. Index numbers are color-coded: Green (0–50 is good), Yellow (51–100 is moderate), Orange (101–150 is unhealthy for sensitive groups), Red (151–200 is unhealthy), Purple (201–300 is very unhealthy), and Maroon (301–500 is hazardous). It is important to keep in mind that high index numbers can occur all year long. What is more, an argument could be made that the designated levels—what is considered unhealthy—should be more stringent.

Weather apps on cell phones may include AQI numbers for some locations. Another site, World Air Quality Index, measures hourly air pollution across the globe. You can compare the AQI number in your area to other cities, states, and countries. While different places face unique challenges due to topography and other factors—more air quality efforts may be needed to address air pollution levels in landlocked areas with heavy traffic than on islands, for instance—it is critical to understand that if index levels are high, our health is in danger, and immediate actions are necessary.

Generally, countries such as Sweden, Norway, Finland, New Zealand, and Iceland, among others, rank well on AQI data. Note that not all countries use the same measurement system. Canada uses Air Quality Health Index (a range of 1–10+), much of Europe uses Common Air Quality Index (0–100), United Kingdom uses Daily Air Quality Index (1–10), the Netherlands use LKI (1–11), and so on.

Where I live in the Midwestern United States, we experience AQI alerts throughout the year, often with an AQI color-code of Orange, meaning over 100 and unhealthy for sensitive groups. In fact, at the time of this writing, Indianapolis had received an F report card rating from the American Lung Association for particle pollution. Check the American Lung Association website to view a report card for your city or state. This organization also lists ways to protect yourself when AQI levels are high.

Despite air quality alerts (referred to as Air Quality Action Days or Knozone Action Days in some areas) not everyone heeds the safety recommendations. When the AQI is Orange (unhealthy for sensitive groups), for example, people should postpone using gas-powered lawn equipment and refueling cars until after 7:00 p.m. People are also advised to turn down air conditioners, opt to bike, walk, use public transportation, or carpool rather than drive solo, and limit outdoor activities. But I've noticed lawn crews operating their gas-powered mowing equipment and children engaged in outdoor activities despite high AQI numbers and warnings that the air is unhealthy. At other times, AQI alerts indicate that the outdoor air quality is very unhealthy or hazardous for everyone in that location. In those situations, it may be necessary to wear a mask or stay indoors. Yet, even during the high levels of particle pollution from the Canadian wildfires, some people—including young children—were outdoors in extremely poor air quality conditions. Perhaps we have not done enough to educate our communities about air quality pollution risks.

Lowering air pollution levels means working to reduce fossil fuel pollution from vehicles, industries, and power plants—which will also address climate change. Things we can do as individuals include walking, bicycling, and using clean energy public transportation plus contacting legislators to ensure our energy is generated using renewable energy sources, such as solar, wind, geothermal, and hydropower. An excellent source of information about air pollution health hazards and action steps we can take is found on the Moms Clean Air Force website; this organization protects children from air pollution and climate change.

Collectively, we can demand that the air we breathe is healthy. We can also VOTE for people who are working to protect our planet, who care about our health, and who are safeguarding our Earth home for future generations.

BANNING FOSSIL FUEL ADS

When scientific research linked cigarette smoking to respiratory diseases, the United States put restrictions on tobacco advertisements in 1971. Research had shown that cigarette advertising increased consumption. Likewise, we know that burning fossil fuels creates harmful air pollution and that air pollution can lead to lung disease, heart disease, and respiratory disorders. Per a study cited by Harvard T.H. Chan School of Public Health, fine particle air pollution from burning fossil fuels resulted in more than 8 million premature deaths, killing about one in five people worldwide. ("Global Mortality From Outdoor Fine Particle Pollution Generated by Fossil Fuel Combustion," published in Environmental Research.) As a result, health professionals and organizations are speaking out about the public health hazards from fossil fuel pollution. As stated in an article in the Global Climate and Health Alliance:

> More than 1,000 health professionals and 200 health organizations from around the world have today called on governments to urgently develop and implement a Fossil Fuel Non-Proliferation Treaty to end global dependence on fossil fuels, in order to protect the health of people around the world. The World Health Organi-

zation, the International Pediatric Association, the World Medical Association, the Alliance of Nurses for a Healthy Environment, and the World Federation of Public Health Associations are amongst the signatories of a letter that demands that governments lay out a legally binding global plan to phase out fossil fuel use.

We also know that the burning of fossil fuels contributes to climate change. EarthRights International, a nongovernmental nonprofit, and ClientEarth, an environmental charity, assert that oil companies such as Exxon have known for over 40 years about the dangers of climate change from the burning of fossil fuel. ClientEarth claims that Exxon (through documents obtained from its Canadian subsidiary, Imperial Oil Ltd.) was aware that burning fossil fuels increased carbon dioxide in the atmosphere in the 1970s and 1980s, adding, "Since 1998, ExxonMobile is estimated to have spent over $33 million on groups that spread doubt and disinformation about climate change."

As stated by the United Nations, "Misleading the public to believe an organization or entity is doing more to protect the environment than it is," is known as greenwashing. Per the United Nations, "Greenwashing undermines credible efforts to reduce emissions and address the climate crisis." The Environmental Working Group, a nonprofit, nonpartisan organization, cites a US House Oversight and Reform Committee investigation, released in 2022, finding that Big Oil companies engaged in a "long-running greenwashing campaign," while enjoying record profits at the pumps.

Concerned policymakers are taking measures to protect their communities. For example, cities in Europe and Australia are working to ban fossil fuel ads. The city of Sydney, for instance, supports a ban on advertising by companies involved in the production or supply of fossil fuels. Comms Declare, a nonpartisan group of Australian communications professionals who work for a climate-friendly future (along with other news sources), estimate that fossil fuel companies spent approximately $200 million on fossil fuel advertisements and marketing in Australia in one year. They assert that these advertisements cover up the health risks from polluting industries and increase demand for products that harm people's health. France and cities in the Netherlands—such as Amsterdam, the Hague, Utrecht, Leiden, Enschede, and Haarlem—also passed motions to restrict fossil fuel advertising.

We need more people to speak out to protect our health and the health of our planet from the hazards of burning coal, oil, and gas. Moreover, when we see an onslaught of social media posts demonizing a young woman like Greta Thunberg or when we become aware of advertisements that try to make a polluting fossil fuel company look good, just know that there's *a lot* of money at stake and a lot of effort going into protecting fossil fuel industry profits. Anyone who has a family member with lung cancer, a serious respiratory disease, or anyone who has experienced the catastrophic harms from climate-related disasters already understands that our health and well-being matter more than corporate revenues.

DIVESTING FROM FOSSIL FUELS

To help me sleep better at night, I decide to make sure that my retirement account funds are not contributing to climate change. Therefore, I set up an appointment to speak with the investment company that handles my retirement account to let them know I want to divest from fossil fuels and do not want my money supporting these polluting industries.

During the telephone call with my investment adviser, she seems confused about the purpose of my call. Instead, while conducting an annual review of my funds, she tells me that she is not the person who handles socially responsible investing. A follow-up email from her informs me that the person I need to speak to about socially responsible investing no longer works at this investment firm. After calling the 1-800 number listed on the investment firm website and speaking to someone else, I am given the name of yet another person. As I am speaking with this man, he acknowledges that he only has seven months' experience on the job—apparently socially responsible investing is not considered a very high priority by this investment company. He also cannot help me get my money out of fossil fuel investments, and it doesn't appear to even be an option.

My retirement funds have been with this national, well-known investment company for over a decade. I don't know if the issue is that I don't have enough money for them to take my request seriously, or that they want to make it difficult for me to divest from fossil fuels, or that they are affected by legislation—such as recent laws in Texas regarding investment firms that divest from fossil fuels—or that they don't have the mechanisms in place for dealing with my request. It's a simple question: *How do I divest my retirement money from fossil fuel companies?*

Aside from the moral/ethics of socially responsible investing, fossil fuels seem like a bad investment because they are not sustainable as a source of energy. The future is clean energy. Some states may have fears about their economies if people start making decisions not to support polluting industries that are contributing to climate change. But, as mentioned earlier, these harms have been evident for decades. Government leaders and business leaders should have transitioned toward clean renewable energy a long time ago. Meanwhile, some state legislators in the United States are now busy trying to push laws that will punish firms that engage in fossil fuel divestment. Frankly, it is a bullying tactic to control people—and for whose benefit? The wealthy people at multinational fossil fuel companies who support the campaigns of some politicians?

Since the investment company that handles my retirement funds is not able to assist me, I roll up my sleeves and Google, "How to divest from fossil fuels?" I learn that people have made similar ethical decisions in the past. For instance, according to an article in *Time* magazine, "Students at many universities opposed recruitment by firms profiting from the Vietnam War and protested their universities' investments in companies such as Dow Chemical, which made napalm, a jelly gasoline that was used in Vietnam in firebombs and flamethrowers." Today, some universities and cities have already made the smart decision to divest from fossil fuels.

Eventually, I locate a nonprofit organization, As You Sow, which contains a host of information regarding shareholder advocacy. This site indicates that if people can divest from the top 200 or so polluting fossil fuel companies, that can have a significant effect.

After the disappointing runaround regarding my retirement account investments, I speak with another large investment company that also does not offer the option to divest from fossil fuels, but someone there does put me in contact with an individual who could manage my account —for a substantial fee—in a socially responsible manner. That option is too costly. After much searching, I locate a company that offers investment options for divesting from fossil fuels. It will cost a bit more to align my investments with my values, but it is not cost prohibitive. I transfer my retirement funds to this company.

Not everyone has the luxury of owning a retirement account or has the option to divest an account from fossil fuel companies. But during my research, I discover that we can also make a positive difference by selecting banking institutions and credit card companies that do not support fossil fuel companies. Even if we're not in a position to influence financial institutions, we can inquire about the investment priorities of our workplaces, cities, universities, nonprofit organizations, and businesses where we purchase products. If we are able to make investment changes—either as individuals or as stakeholders in organizations and businesses—perhaps other people will follow our lead.

Such actions sometimes require a lot of leg work and a careful assessment of costs, values, and needs. My suggestion: Don't stop at the first roadblock. Find a way around and through to the results you seek.

ENVIRONMENTAL LAWSUITS

Lawsuits are one way to demand accountability for the serious harms caused by fossil fuel companies. In a groundbreaking civil lawsuit, a subsidiary of BP (BP Products North America Inc.) agreed to pay a $40 million penalty to settle charges filed by the U.S. Department of Justice and the Environmental Protection Agency regarding the release of harmful pollutants in the air and in wastewater by the BP Whiting refinery near the shoreline of Lake Michigan.

Around the world, lawsuits have also been filed regarding climate change. Several cities and states throughout the United States, especially in areas facing a high risk of disasters from climate change, have filed lawsuits for harms incurred and/or for disinformation and misleading advertisements. Per a 2023 article in *The*

Guardian, "More than two dozen U.S. cities and states are suing big oil alleging the fossil fuel industry knew for decades about the dangers of burning coal, oil and gas, and actively hid that information from consumers and investors."

Additionally, young people are taking their cases to court to demand responsibility from their governments and/or from the fossil fuel industry. Children are more vulnerable to the health hazards of pollution, and their rights to a heathy climate and healthy life are in danger when businesses or governments fail to take action to tackle climate risks. According to the United Nations Environment Programme (UNEP), over thirty climate litigation cases have been brought by and on behalf of youth under twenty-five years old. As mentioned earlier, the youth in Montana achieved a landmark victory in a lawsuit regarding the risks from climate change and their constitutional right to a clean and healthful environment. (The case is being appealed by the state but, hopefully, will be upheld for the youth).

Findings by UNEP and the Sabin Center for Climate Change Law at Columbia University, "show that climate litigation is becoming an integral part of securing climate action and justice." These legal actions speak to the urgency with which people—both young and old—want accountability for the dangers we are facing from climate change and from environmental pollutants.

CHAPTER SIX
AUTUMN

"We can't solve problems by using the same kind of thinking we used when we created them."

— ALBERT EINSTEIN

CHANGE IS IN THE AIR

An early morning mist lingers above the fields as the bright blaze of sunrise gradually appears over a distant farmhouse. I love visiting Southern Indiana. The wind moves over the dark green fields of soybeans like a gentle caress. If you stand still beside the fields, you can hear the grasshoppers as they leap from plant to plant, their wings buzzing as they fly through the air. In another nearby field, the air rustles sharply through tall cornstalks. Crickets are chirping, and cicadas are buzzing in a low, monotonous vibration that is occasionally broken by the trill of a bird or insect somewhere in the cornfields. An open expanse of blue sky stretches out as far as the eye can see, with only a few puffy white clouds.

As the sun rises higher in the sky, everyone becomes

busy with daily activities. My husband and his mother, Dorothy, are indoors making a peach custard pie with the last of the summer peaches. Russ, my husband's father, is working in the garden. His arms are a burnt dark purple color from his decades in the sun, and he looks thin and a bit frail. He is occupied with digging up potatoes. We are all enjoying the slightly cooler fall weather this week, along with the sunshine. Russ doesn't appear to hear a distant train whistle. I imagine a train waiting for him to climb aboard when he passes. Lately, he has been showing signs of dementia. At ninety-four, perhaps he doesn't need the heavy baggage of memories for the journey ahead. He has definitely lived a full life. Isn't that what we all desire in the end—a few precious moments from a life well lived?

The wind chimes hanging from the tree branch jingle as a breeze blows past.

I hear the deep cadence of a toad and a cicada chorus that once again rolls through the landscape, swelling in pitch and then slowly ebbing. Dry bee balm plants stand tall in the flowerbed. In the garden, a few cantaloupes are waiting to ripen, and one orangish-green tomato remains on the vine. Most vegetation has already been harvested. I glance up at the majestic pecan tree near the lane leading to Russ and Dorothy's farmhouse as I start heading toward the house. I'm looking forward to fresh garden vegetables and a homemade peach custard pie for dessert.

This is a pleasant moment. Yet, change is in the air. Change asks us to be brave. To dare to try something different. To see the new possibilities before us. To grow and to evolve.

A SOLAR-POWERED FUTURE

While there has been some debate in rural communities regarding the pros and cons of solar panel farms, organizations such as the NAACP see opportunities for progress and growth in renewable energy.

Community-owned solar, for instance, allows people who would otherwise not be able to afford solar panels on their roofs to co-own a solar project. They can then receive credits on their bills for energy generated that they share with other customers. James Mosley, chair of the Environment & Climate Justice Committee for the NAACP's Evansville, Indiana, branch and owner of EnviroKinetics, says, "Promoting alternative energy and green-collar jobs should be part of a national urban policy, with infrastructure projects that serve to provide equity and resilience for residents in marginalized communities."

As the NAACP states, "Low-income and communities of color have suffered disproportionate harm from the fossil fuel economy. The new clean energy economy is an opportunity to address past injustices." Per its website, the NAACP envisions a solar-powered future that invests in under-resourced communities, creates local, sustainable wealth, and adds to community resilience and a healthier future for all. Toward that effort, the NAACP would like investor-owned utilities to offer community-owned solar programs.

Innovative companies, and cities, are utilizing solar panel community projects in combination with ecosystem restoration to revitalize dilapidated urban spaces. In some cases, solar panel projects are just one part of a larger, comprehensive eco-friendly initiative that adds native plants, green spaces for children to play, and walking paths. Earlier this year, I attended an environmental resiliency conference where a representative from Stantec, a company that advances sustainability designs for communities, mentioned Grand Ridge Solar Farm in north central Illinois that incorporates native prairie to promote pollinator habitat. Another solar project in

LaGrange, Georgia, includes pollinator vegetation. Some solar projects have also included the planting of native plants underneath the solar panels to bring in more pollinators to help with crops.

Schools are also adopting green programs that include solar panels. For example, Shakamak Jr./Sr. High School in Indiana's Wabash Valley has installed a solar panel farm that will save the school over $1 million in twelve years. They also incorporate green energy into the students' curriculum and career opportunities.

According to the World Economic Forum, many cities in the United States are utilizing solar power. Examples include Honolulu, Hawaii; Las Vegas, Nevada; San Diego, California; Albuquerque, New Mexico; San Jose, California; San Antonio, Texas; and Burlington, Vermont, to name only a few. Citing the Environment America Research & Policy Center, Shining Cities 2022 report, local governments should "establish goals for 100% renewable energy and create roadmaps and programs to achieve those goals."

ENVIRONMENTAL JUSTICE

To learn more about environmental justice and equity, I am attending the Richard M. Fairbanks Environmental Justice Symposium, an all-day presentation led by Black community leaders. A key point from the panel of speakers is that taking care of our environment is not just about saving trees, oceans, and polar bears. Our environment is where we live, it is our bodies, and it is our neighborhoods. The Merriam-Webster dictionary defines environment as the circumstances, objects, and conditions by which one is surrounded. It can also be the climate, soil, and living things that act upon an organism or an ecological community, as well as the aggerate of social and cultural conditions that influence the life of an individual or community.

How we define environment matters because we must not overlook marginalized communities when we talk about the protection, health, and care of our Earth home. We also do not want to ignore impoverished communities across the globe that are facing some of the harshest effects from climate change.

The morning speakers at the Environmental Justice Symposium emphasize that understanding the history of racism in relation to how we care for our environment is critical. For instance, Kaila Austin, a public historian, artist, and community activist, tells the story of historically Black neighborhoods—Norwood and Lovetown—where originally there were forests and old-growth orchards with fruit trees. She learned from the elders in this community during her oral history project that they used to go to the orchard to pick apples and pears along with rhubarb and grapes. As she says, the community lived off the land. Then, in the early 1900s, a hazardous coal-fuel utility plant was built.

Later, highway projects further divided Black communities, making collective activism difficult. Industrial factories razed the land and deposited toxins. From there, water quality suffered, and residents lived in unhealthy conditions. As the panelists point out, "You can't do anything on toxic land." Another panelist sums up the discussion, saying, "We have to reckon with our history of racism in order to untangle the legacy of racism in our environmental policies." The speakers agree that in the United States, we have a toxic heritage regarding our environmental policies for Black communities.

Later in the day, Paula Brooks, environmental justice director for the Hoosier Environmental Council, says, "We all want clean, safe, healthy neighborhoods." The individuals on the afternoon panel explain that we need to respect the residents' agency to know what they need in their neighborhoods. The people living in their communities know their history, and they know their assets. She states that Black neighborhoods can serve as significant resources, and they are communities of power. As Paula suggests to those in attendance, "Make friends with people who are vastly different from you are." We must, she adds, learn from one another.

A youth representative, Chioh Mwaafrika from the Kheprw Institute—a grassroots community organization focused on youth leadership and community empowerment—says that we need to dig deeper and get to the root cause of our environmental problems. Some of these roots include poverty, classism, class disparity, and redlining. For those unfamiliar with the term, redlining arose out of the segregation policies in the United States where mortgage lenders, through discriminatory practices, refused to insure home mortgages in or near Black neighborhoods. Another panel member notes that a major root problem is that the people in local government, as public servants, should not be harming people through environmental policies that negatively impact disadvantaged communities.

Per another panel member, environmental harms, such as water pollution, pose even greater problems for people in poor communities. He says that individuals in these neighborhoods, often made up of racial and ethnic minorities, are fishing in water polluted with E. coli to obtain their main food source. Awhile back, I saw a TikTok video where lots of children and families were swimming at Belle Isle Beach on the Detroit River in Michigan, even though the beach was closed due to high levels of E. coli. The people interviewed said they didn't see the warning signs, or they didn't know that the reason for the closure was related to health risks and assumed that it was fine because there were so many people swimming. The bigger question, of course, is why the swimming or fishing areas for predominantly Black families are so polluted that it puts their health at risk just to go fishing or go for a swim on a sweltering hot day.

After identifying the root problems, the speakers at the Environmental Justice Symposium state that we then need to implement solutions that come from the people: not solutions *for* the people but *from* the people. Paula agrees. "Justice is the goal."

ADVOCACY

This afternoon, I sit down with Amanda Shepherd, Sierra Club deputy regional field director, to talk about climate change. The Sierra Club is a grassroots environmental organization in the United States with more than three million members and supporters. It was founded in 1892 by the conservationist John Muir. Sierra Club groups are active in various states working on environmental justice issues, energy, conservation, water protection, and the climate crisis.

In addition to her role at the Sierra Club, Amanda "walks the talk" in her personal life and demonstrates an ongoing deep passion for the love and protection of our Earth home. She and her husband installed beautiful solar panels in their yard, because their house roof is small and shaded. They also put together a landscaping plan, including native plants, to ensure that the panels would not be visible from the road, and they obtained permits from the city for the solar panels. Amanda's home is in an urban neighborhood. Instead of rewarding these efforts to mitigate climate change, several neighbors opposed the solar panels, and the city revoked the permits and then scheduled zoning variance hearings.

I don't know why people fight so hard to keep the status quo or prefer to go backward when it comes to making progress on issues concerning the health of our environment. Evolution is a good thing, and when it comes to protecting our Earth, maintaining the status quo is not an option. (After my talk with Amanda, she and her husband had the solar panels removed from their yard because of the neighborhood opposition, and they have since moved to a new neighborhood.)

I ask Amanda what we can do to help address climate change. She says advocacy is critical. We need to contact our local and state representatives and become informed and educated on issues such as the climate. She emphasizes that we need the power grid to move toward renewables. Per Amanda, it's important to get beyond dirty fuels like coal by moving toward climate-friendly green energy solutions, such as solar. She is a strong advocate for our Earth, working diligently in the community to protect our planet and the health of future generations.

In good news, my neighbors put solar panels on their roof, and I've also noticed on my walks a number of "carbon neutral" signs popping up in people's yards. Another homeowner in a nearby neighborhood put solar panels in their yard. In not-so-good news, I went past a new community housing development—with newly constructed homes—and not one roof had solar panels, despite being in direct sunlight because the developers took out all the trees.

Housing and commercial building developers could do so much better to help with climate change by installing solar panels and/or other alternative sources of clean energy, putting in extra insulation, utilizing energy-efficient appliances, and keeping mature trees. Of course, rehabbing existing buildings to improve blighted neighborhoods and business districts is preferable to the clear-cutting of urban forests just to put up expensive new housing. Regrettably, in Indiana, the state government no longer offers incentives for adding solar panels to buildings, an example of moving backward rather than forward.

Fortunately, on the federal level in the United States, there is excellent news to report with the Inflation Reduction Act. Per The Nature Conservancy, "The Inflation Reduction Act of 2022 includes around $370 billion in clean energy and climate investments over the next ten years that represent the most significant climate action taken by Congress ever." (Visit The Nature Conservancy website for a fact-sheet regarding the benefits of this landmark bill.) Earthjustice, a nonprofit public interest environmental law organization, also has a summary that highlights the climate solutions afforded by the Inflation Reduction Act, stating, "The bill will put us on a path to 40% emissions reduction by 2030 while restoring U.S. credibility to lead climate action on the global stage." The Inflation Reduction Act also makes solar more affordable for homeowners, nonprofit organizations, and community solar projects and will benefit low-income and disadvantaged communities.

SOLAR UNITED NEIGHBORS

A national organization helping people gain access to solar power and advocating for people's energy rights is Solar United Neighbors, a nonprofit organization working to bring the benefits of solar energy to local communities. To hear more about their efforts, I am speaking with Zach Schalk, Indiana program director, at a neighborhood coffeehouse. According to Zach, Solar United Neighbors (SUN) started when two twelve-year-old friends, Walter and Diego, asked their parents to put solar panels on their homes in Washington, D.C. The boys had just watched the Al Gore movie, *An Inconvenient Truth*, and wanted to help fight climate change. Because it was expensive, they signed up forty-five other neighbors, forming the city's first solar co-op. Other neighboring communities then wanted to duplicate their success. In response, Walter's mom, Anya Schoolman, started SUN, with a mission to help communities obtain a clean, equitable energy system.

As Zach explains, there are lots of benefits to going solar, such as saving on energy bills, increasing the resale value of a home, and reducing greenhouse gas emissions that contribute to climate change. SUN is a community resource for how to do so, offering a free solar help desk with an expert to assist with answering questions, along with up-to-date information that guides people through solar installation options and a competitive bidding process to connect consumers to solar installers. As Zach says, "We give people information to make decisions that are right for them."

With a national grassroots network of over 500,000 solar supporters, SUN utilizes education and advocacy to fight for the rights of homeowners, schools, businesses, and other community members to go solar. Zach says, "We are a resource for everyone, and we fight for better policies. But we need everyone to speak up because policy barriers can otherwise make solar power access more difficult." Indiana, for instance, eliminated net metering for new solar owners. Net metering had previously allowed residential solar owners to receive a fair credit on their electric bill for excess solar generation at the full retail value for that electricity.

Zach emphasizes that we have to join efforts to educate legislators and speak up so that all people can benefit from solar as a climate solution. He says, "We need to be resilient for situations like power outages. It's a nonpartisan issue when people want to go solar: whether they don't like electric monopolies, or they want a safe energy source during outages, or they want to fight climate change." He adds, "We want to help everyone, regardless of the reasons for wanting to go solar."

He refers me to a recent success story in Minnesota where legislators passed policies that will increase access to solar energy across the state. The aim is to move Minnesota to 100 percent clean energy by 2040. A new law prohibits homeowners associations from blocking rooftop solar, and a Solar Rewards program will reward customers for the solar power they produce. There are also dedicated funds to help low-income communities go solar and a fund to help schools go solar as well.

Today, SUN has people across the United States assisting schools, congregations, neighborhoods, individuals, nonprofits, and businesses to make solar the cornerstone of a modern clean energy system. The organization's website contains a wealth of valuable information and is a great resource for people who want to know more about how to install solar power or how to speak with representatives to ensure that solar power is a viable option for everyone in the community. SUN believes that a more just and equitable future means bringing solar opportunities back to the community.

CREATIVE SOLAR INNOVATIONS

While in Miami with my daughter, mentioned earlier, I happened to see outdoor solar "trees" at a museum park near where I was staying. Rather than only being placed on building rooftops, these metal structures are shaped like trees with solar panels on top. They don't replace the need to plant real trees; they serve as a way to generate solar power rather than relying on fossil fuels.

According to Spotlight Solar's website, Florida Power & Light's SolarNow program utilizes solar trees and solar canopies at parks, museums, zoos, and other locations to provide shade while also generating emissions-free solar energy. These solar innovations are used primarily in commercial settings and often include artistic design flares that make them eye-catching.

A world-famous display combining solar energy with artistic design is located in Singapore at the Gardens by the Bay, where solar-powered Supertrees up to 160 feet tall act as vertical gardens for over 160,000 plants. Per its website, Gardens by the Bay is based on principles of environmental sustainability, such as carbon-neutral electricity generated on-site and energy-efficient solutions in cooling. Its conservatories, for instance, utilize displacement cooling: chilled water pipes in the floor slabs provide cooling while warm air rises and is vented out at high levels.

Another recent innovative cooling system, called the Cartuja Qanat project, is found in Seville, Spain, a country that has experienced dangerous heat extremes. Instead of burning fossil fuels that contribute to increased planet warming, this architectural experiment is inspired by Persians who realized 1,000 years ago that canal waters brought through tunnels cooled the air and that this cooler air could be brought to the surface with vertical shafts. The Cartuja Qanat structure uses an underground system where the water is cooled; solar-powered pumps then draw the cooled water up through vertical pipes and cold air is vented out. This architectural project also incorporates green spaces and open-air spaces, among other sustainability solutions to address a warming planet. (Completion of this pioneering project was on hold at the time of this writing).

During the pandemic, we learned how connected we are globally. We also know from current events that a war, disease, or an uprising anywhere can affect our food supply chain as well as things like the cost of gasoline or the cost of fuel for heating or cooling our living spaces. Independent local sources of energy, such as solar, are needed. Even during the hurricane in Florida, one of the communities that relies on solar—Babcock Ranch—fared better than the neighboring areas because they did not lose their source of electricity.

Many cities and countries are finding ways to implement climate-ready green solutions, such as solar panels being placed on bus stop shelters, business buildings, hospitals, schools, museums, and so on. These advances demonstrate that creativity and innovation can work hand-in-hand to find bold ways to move society forward using clean energy sources.

In time, perhaps, solar will be the primary way of lighting our urban areas. If you have ever seen an aerial view of a city lit-up at night, it is readily apparent that we desperately need to implement clean energy alternatives for our massive energy consumption in the United States and elsewhere in the world.

FAITH-BASED SOLUTIONS

Many faith-based groups—Buddhist, Christian, Jewish, Baha'i, Unitarian Universalist, Sikh, Muslim, Hindu, Indigenous, Centers for Spiritual Living, Pagan, Goddess, and other religious affiliations—have adopted Earth care measures to reduce their carbon footprint and alleviate climate change. These faith-based calls-to-action are leading the way on sustainable Earth stewardship practices. Of course, Earth-based religions and Indigenous Peoples have been honoring the care of our Earth for centuries.

More recently, Pope Francis voiced his strong public

position regarding the climate change crisis threatening our common Earth home and our moral obligation to care for the poor who are adversely affected. In a letter called Laudato Si—which is a reference to a prayer from the pope's namesake, St. Francis, the patron saint of ecology—the pope declared that the science of climate change is clear and must be addressed to protect the Earth and everyone on it. As a result, Catholics are heeding his words and taking necessary actions to ensure they protect our Earth home.

Thich Nhat Hanh, in the Buddhist tradition, called for mindful Earth stewardship with his book *Love Letter to the Earth*. His message is that the Earth is not something outside of us, it is part of us. He said all the elements that make up our bodies come from the Earth. It is not just the environment we live in: "We are the Earth." He emphasized that we must love Mother Earth if the Earth is to survive. Mindfully, we must each do our part to demonstrate love, compassion, and care for our Mother Earth.

Other religious denominations also have adopted measures to help take care of our Earth. For instance, Ray Wilson, an engineer and solar advocate, helped spearhead sustainability actions at his Unitarian Universalist Church of Indianapolis. This church group installed solar panels on the roof and on the ground, reducing the energy use on the property by 40 percent, in addition to generating most of the church building's electrical requirements. As noted by the Environmental Resilience Institute, over fifty Indiana congregations of various faith traditions have installed solar panels on their buildings.

Science of Mind magazine, a Centers for Spiritual Living publication that I contribute articles to on occasion, uses recycled paper for its magazine, along with other sustainability measures in its global community. It can cost more to go this route—depending on the availability of recycled paper supplies and unforeseeable situations such as fires. But it's another good example of a faith community that is putting its Earth care values into beneficial actions. Quakers are likewise active in Earth care measures with an Earth Quaker Action Team (EQAT), a nonviolent, grassroots action group fighting for a sustainable, just economy.

These are just a few examples of the *numerous* faith-based organizations across the globe that are implementing Earth stewardship measures. Some of these eco-friendly actions include planting trees and native flowers, starting organic food gardens, installing solar panels, eliminating single-use plastics, implementing recycling programs, and tackling environmental equity and climate justice issues through educational programs. Places of worship also host Earth Day events, farmers' markets, environmental speakers, vegan lunches, and Earth-themed art exhibits. These green team or creation care initiatives are impressively encouraging. Importantly, some leaders in the faith community are speaking out for renewable energy, clean drinking water, and eradication of toxic pollutants in their local communities.

Faith-based groups can be inspirational trailblazers in their communities, demonstrating through their actions a reverence for God's creation and a love for our shared Earth. For places of worship in the United States that would like to learn more about Earth stewardship and climate action, Interfaith Power & Light is a nonprofit organization with resources and educational programs for the faith community. Internationally, the United Nations Faith for Earth Initiative has useful resources.

All of these eco-friendly activities in our religious and spiritual communities serve to remind us that it's vital for people everywhere to protect our Earth home and care for all who live here.

A LAND STEWARDSHIP MISSION

This morning, I am visiting Reverend Amber Good, director of education at Teter Retreat and Organic Farm, an outreach mission of Noblesville First United Methodist Church. Amber is an interpretive naturalist at the farm and has an Advanced Master Naturalist certificate. She also has a degree from Purdue University's School of Agriculture in wildlife science with a minor in environmental science, and she has master's degrees in divinity and theological studies.

When I arrive at Teter Farm, Amber explains a bit of the farm's history. Back in 2016, Pastor Aaron Hobbs had a vision of utilizing land that had been left to the church as an organic farm to feed mind, body, and spirit. The mission of Teter Farm became to increase access to healthy food for the vulnerable and to provide ecological education while building relationships and community. The farm, with 120 acres along the White River, now grows produce for local food banks, which distribute the produce to food pantries and feeding programs. Amber says the primary goal is food security and healthy living.

While walking the farm grounds, I notice a group of volunteers assembling a hoop house (there are six so far); these hoop houses help to extend the growing season. The farm has rows of vegetables along with native flower gardens, an orchard with fruit trees, chickens, beehives off in the distance, a wooded area with old-growth trees and hiking paths, an outdoor worship area, and a retreat house.

I hear birdsong overhead and, glancing up, I see several birds swooping over the fields. Farm manager Katy Rogers explains that the farm has a killdeer bird sanctuary with mulched mounds where these particular birds like to lay their eggs. Amber adds that the birds also eat unwanted bugs, which is helpful because they do not spray any pesticides. Amber says, "We are working *with* nature. This is the way it should be: people living with the Earth and in relationship to it and not opposed to it."

Teter Farm also offers Community Supported Agriculture (CSA) as a way for people in the community to purchase certified organic vegetables directly from the farm and enjoy the benefits of eating seasonal, healthy produce: vegetables grown from non-GMO seed without the use of synthetic fertilizers or pesticides. The CSA program supports the farm's ability to donate healthy produce to feed those in need.

Amber says that when people ask, "What does Christianity have to do with the land?" her response is, "Stewardship of the land has *everything* to do with God and our spiritual practices." As Teter Farm makes evident, faith communities are uniquely positioned to contribute significantly to the care of our Earth and to the care of those individuals and families who are most in need of healthy food programs. For instance, according to Yale Climate Connections, the Roman Catholic Church owns 177 million acres of land around the world, and some of that land could be put to use to benefit people, wildlife, and our Earth, while also working toward combatting climate change.

Faith communities around the world are following the call to be good Earth stewards. Teter Farm is just one example where people of faith are utilizing their resources in service of humanity and in loving care of our Earth home.

GREEN ROOFS

On a trip to visit family in Chicago, Illinois, I happen to observe from the apartment balcony an abundance of green vegetation covering a nearby rooftop. Doing a bit of research, I learn that, in fact, Chicago's City Hall has a green roof, as do a number of other buildings throughout the city. According to Midstory, a nonprofit media organization, "Today, the City Hall rooftop features more than 150 species of plants and 20,000 individual plants, most native to the Chicago region. Its bees produce 200 pounds of honey every year." The City Hall green roof also reduces energy costs and mitigates the effects of urban heat islands. Throughout the city, green roofs are being used on schools, police stations, libraries, firehouses, restaurants, and, in some cases, to grow herbs and organic produce.

Green roof projects in North American cities can be found in Washington, D.C., Newark, New York City, Toronto, Seattle, Portland, Philadelphia, Culpeper, and Gaithersburg, to name only a few. Indianapolis has some green roof buildings as well. For example, Juan Solomon Park—named after a civic leader in the Black community—incorporates sustainability features into a forty-one-acre urban park, including a green roof, a playground surfaced with recycled rubber tires, nature trails, and a lift station to manage sewage overflow. Other green roofs in the city can be found at The Children's Museum, The Nature Conservancy, Keep Indianapolis Beautiful, WFYI Public Media, Butler University, and the Sidney & Lois Eskenazi Hospital.

When I return from Chicago, I visit the Sidney & Lois Eskenazi hospital rooftop, called The Sky Farm. They have planted carrots, zucchini, tomatoes, eggplants, cabbage, kale, broccoli, cucumbers, beets, peas, celery, lettuce, green beans, collards, potatoes, peppers, turnips, radishes, and a variety of herbs. They also have a beehive! It's a wonderful model of holistic health and healing for the community.

The University of Notre Dame has Indiana's largest living green roof project, with 122,000 square feet of vegetation on top of five buildings. These green roofs "mitigate stormwater run-off, improve air quality by reducing carbon dioxide, provide noise insulation, naturally insulate to keep indoor temperatures lower during warm months and higher in cold months, and conserve rainwater for release back into the atmosphere," according to the university website. In addition to its impressive eco-friendly green roofs, the University of Notre Dame has adopted several sustainability projects in response to Pope Francis's letter asking everyone to care for our common home. In an effort to cut its carbon footprint and be good Earth stewards, Notre Dame uses solar and geothermal energy, LED lighting, and LEED building certifications on all new construction. Significantly, the university ceased burning coal years ago and, more recently, partnered with the city of South Bend on a new hydroelectric facility. The Earth care measures throughout the campus are remarkable.

Countries outside of the United States—such as Germany, Japan, Canada, Singapore, and Switzerland, for instance—plus Hong Kong, have green roofs on many of their buildings, and some of these green roof projects date back to the 1960s. In an effort to fight climate change, cities around the world are also enacting policies to ensure that new construction includes sustainability measures like green roofs or solar panels. A few examples of such policies can be found in Toronto, Basel, Tokyo, Munich, Copenhagen, and Zurich. Numerous cities also provide incentives for green roofs through tax rebates, refunds, and favorable zoning policies.

The U.S. Environmental Protection Agency's (EPA) website contains excellent information regarding the enormous environmental and health benefits of green roofs, along with an example of an extensive green roof project on the EPA headquarter building in Denver, Colorado.

It is encouraging to see Earth-friendly innovations being applied in places across the globe by civic leaders who care about their communities and the well-being of Mother Earth.

OUR MODES OF TRANSPORTATION

I grew up in Michigan, birthplace of Henry Ford, the founder of Ford Motor company. My stepfather, along with many people in our neighborhood, worked at factory jobs in the automobile industry. I also lived, worked, and went to law school in Detroit, known as the Motor City for its role as the global center of the American automotive industry. Now, I reside in Indiana, where the Indianapolis 500 at the Indianapolis Motor Speedway is a famous destination for car racing fans who travel from across the country to watch the race.

The infrastructure and mindset in much of the United States is definitely based on a car-centric culture. Hollywood movies, advertisements, and celebrity magazines have showcased vehicles as symbols of prestige since the early 1900s. Even today, automobile advertisements highlight full-sized vehicles roaming the landscape in search of epic adventures. Across the United States, we continue to build more and more highways and currently have the largest road network in the world. I saw a Facebook post pointing out that instead of saying, "a deer is in the road" or "a deer is crossing the road," we might more accurately say, "A road has been paved over the deer's habitat." Heavy traffic and vehicle emissions contribute to our air pollution problems. As already noted, air pollution has a significant effect on public health: the cars, trucks, and buses using dirty fossil fuels on our roads put both our health and our Earth in peril.

In my present neighborhood, grocery stores are located on busy roads without sidewalks for bikes or pedestrians. Some of us might prefer to walk or bike more, rather than driving, if there were safe, accessible paths to local businesses. Meanwhile, mammoth gas-guzzling vehicles dominate daily road travel here. At drive-through coffee shops, fast food restaurants, and pharmacy pick-up windows, vehicles are frequently left idling for long periods while exhaust fumes fill the air. I recently walked past city-owned utility trucks that were all left empty and idling while the workers were busy fixing a junction box.

Electric cars have existed since the late 1800s, and hydrogen fuel cars were made in the 1960s. Why haven't we moved faster toward energy-efficient vehicles and clean energy public transportation in the United States? Electric cars are a step in the right direction. A friend of mine owns an electric car, and he has been posting on social media how it fares on long trips. To date, he is happy with his purchase. I purchased a hybrid vehicle over a decade ago and saved enormously on fuel costs. Unfortunately, Indiana charges people who own hybrid or electric vehicles an additional fee for license plate registration. Again, this discourages rather than encourages responsible care of our environment and disregards the health of the people who live and work in this state. Of course, electric vehicles are not a complete solution for states, such as Indiana, that obtain the majority of their electricity from dirty fossil fuels such as coal-burning and natural gas plants.

To help our environment, states need to transition to clean, renewable energy sources—such as solar, wind, and geothermal—while putting in place the infrastructure for electric car charging stations. States could also offer incentives to make clean energy choices feasible for consumers and create more clean energy public transportation options, along with having bicycle and walking paths.

Not long ago, on a visit to see my daughter who lives in the Netherlands, I observed *a lot* of bicycles and tiny electric cars, with numerous electric charging stations. There is tremendous respect in cities such as Amsterdam for bicycle riders. In some areas, bicycles are given the right of way over cars, and everyone—from the old to the young—ride bikes to reach their daily destinations, even in inclement weather. Beyond promoting the use of bicycles and electric cars, the mayor of Amsterdam, Femke Halsema, also has a climate neutrality plan with an aim to move toward 100 percent sustainably generated energy, eliminating the use of natural gas and working for traffic to become emission-free. As the former Dutch Climate and Energy Policy minister Rob Jetten stated, "We are working (toward) a completely climate-neutral and circular economy. . . . For that we really have to wean ourselves off fossil fuels and reduce our greenhouse gas emissions."

When people travel on longer trips in the Netherlands, and elsewhere in Europe, public transportation is readily available, and some of that public transportation is also transitioning to clean energy. In the Netherlands, for instance, passenger trains are primarily powered by wind energy. Other places throughout Europe—and in countries such as Australia and India—are beginning to utilize solar-powered, electric, and/or battery-powered trains. Most people would probably love to travel in a rail system that is environmentally friendly, affordable, and comfortable. As I've said before, I can imagine eating a healthy meal, reading a book, and sitting back to relax, perhaps napping in a sleeper train bed for long train trips.

Admittedly, I have to fly via a plane in order to visit my daughter in Europe. For some of us, our loved ones, our jobs, or our educational programs require us to travel long distances. Furthermore, we gain so much valuable knowledge by immersing ourselves in other cultures.

Unfortunately, the majority of airplane travel options do not yet use an environmentally friendly fuel source and instead rely on fossil fuels that contribute to our climate crisis. Airports are, however, making progress toward eco-friendly transportation services, such as installing solar panels to generate power for their facilities. India's Cochin International Airport, for instance, became the world's first solar-powered airport. Indianapolis International Airport has one of the largest airport-based solar farms in the world. Technological advances are also rapidly evolving toward climate-friendly fuel alternatives for airplane transportation. A grand achievement, Icelandair celebrated its first commercial 100 percent electric-powered airplane flight in 2022. Let's hope all airlines adopt clean energy alternatives soon. For the time being, I purchase carbon offsets for my airplane transportation.

As individuals, we can do our best to support industry and government leaders who are adopting the necessary clean energy innovations so that we can continue to travel while not harming our planet. Couldn't we redirect dirty fossil fuel jobs toward renewable energy transportation jobs, creating mass transportation options that benefit the planet, the people, and the economy? We don't have to abandon communities that have historically depended on fossil fuel jobs to support their families; rather, we need to listen to what the people in these communities need to move forward in healthy ways. Perhaps during the transition period, people need job training opportunities and reassurance that they won't lose their retirement plans. As previously stated by James Mosley of the Evansville NAACP, we need green energy jobs that "provide equity and resilience for residents in marginalized communities."

Surely, when we make up our minds to do great things, we can get them accomplished. If we can travel to the moon, we can find ways to travel here on Mother Earth without polluting the air we breathe and the air our children breathe. This time in our history—right now—*could be* an exciting shift toward creativity, innovation, and momentous accomplishments! Perhaps by the time you read this book, we will already have made tremendous strides toward making this dream a reality.

CHAPTER SEVEN

A LOVE OF TREES

"Trees are sanctuaries. Whoever knows how to speak to them, whoever knows how to listen to them, can learn the truth."

— HERMANN HESSE, NOVELIST

MOMENTS OF AWE

It's late autumn in the Midwest. Acorns and walnuts are dropping from the trees, landing loudly on the porch roof and on the ground below the tree branches. Meanwhile, high above the tree tops, a turkey vulture glides past. A large buck showed up in the yard yesterday morning to feast on the abundance of fallen acorns. Today, other than the falling nuts, it's quiet. No squirrels or chipmunks are in sight.

Because of the leafy tree shade—and maybe because of the sun's angle—the tree leaves look dark amid mottled shadows, even though the sky is vivid blue without clouds. The berries on the pokeweed plant are deep purple and mostly gone, leaving a blood red stem, a nice addition of color in an otherwise muted green landscape since the leaves have not yet turned their fall hues of bright orange, red, and yellow.

Listening more intently, I hear the soft buzz of crickets.

The leaves wave in the gentle breeze, and then, all of a sudden, the branches sway with more vigor as a whoosh of wind blows through. Soon after, all is calm again.

Softly, the leaves whisper: *"Spend just a few moments in awe."*

Pausing, I give thanks to the birds, the hum of insects, the breeze, the trees, the smell of mulch, the dried flower stems, the clover beneath my feet, and the shadows cast by the midday sun. I take a deep breath.

A monarch butterfly flutters nearby, as if to say, *"Yes, this is what you should do each day. This will be your prayer, our prayer, and our remembering."*

SAVING URBAN FORESTS

While watching an afternoon rain shower, I hear one lone bird persistently chirping somewhere in the yard. Outside, the leaves remain drab, without much color—even though it's now late October. The seasons flow by "like a broken down dam," to quote John Prine from his song, "Angel from Montgomery."

I've read that the trees were stressed this past year due to drought conditions. Maybe, like people who are exhausted from these challenging times, the trees simply don't have the energy reserves to show their usual vibrant colors. Is this a reminder for us all that if we don't take care of ourselves and our planet, we will not be able to shine brightly in the days to come?

Later in the day, I meet with Rae Schnapp, PhD, director of conservation at the Indiana Forest Alliance (IFA), a nonprofit working to protect the state's forests, including urban forests. Rae explains that trees are critical for lots of reasons! Forests combat climate change by removing carbon from the air. Trees also help clean the air and water of pollutants, prevent soil erosion, absorb flood-waters, and serve as habitat for living creatures, such as bats that roost in a variety of trees for protection and shelter.

She says, "Historically, 80 to 90 percent of our local forests have been destroyed since the 1900s. These areas served as corridors for species migration and, today, several endangered bats are likely to go extinct." Currently, the IFA is conducting "Ecoblitzes," a comprehensive survey to document the biological diversity of plants, insects, and animals that depends on forests for their survival, with special emphasis on pollinators, crustaceans, spiders, amphibians, reptiles, and mammals, including our endangered bats.

What is more, trees and vegetation, as mentioned earlier, cool the environment and reduce urban heat islands. According to Earth.Org, a leading environmental news site, urban heat islands are caused when black asphalt, concrete, dark rooftops, and tall building in urban areas absorb large amounts of heat from the sun, which is "exacerbated by heat emitted from the high concentration of automobile and industrial emissions in cities." The close proximity between buildings also stifles air flow, and the concrete and dark surfaces keep nighttime temperatures higher than normal.

We've witnessed extreme heat waves across the globe and deaths from record-breaking high temperatures. Per Earth.Org, "In general, heat waves kill more people than hurricanes, tornadoes, or floods." Trees not only provide cooling shade but also lower temperatures as they release water vapor. Water is absorbed from the roots to pores on the leaves, where moisture is then released into the atmosphere. Preserving urban forests, planting trees, and saving trees from clear-cutting by industry, excessive logging, and highway expansion projects—especially in low-income neighborhoods—is lifesaving work for us all.

Finally, forests supply a source of beauty where people can connect with nature, which benefits our physical and mental well-being. As scientists in Japan found, spending time in a forest's atmosphere, also called "forest bathing," lowers blood pressure and stress hormone levels. Likewise in the United Kingdom, scientists found that people who spend time in nature report significantly greater health and well-being.

On my way home after meeting with Rae, I pass by a large wooded lot with For Sale signs posted in each of the plots being subdivided for expensive housing. Sadly, it's not the first time a beautiful wooded area is put on the chopping block in the interest of profit-making. Developers seem intent on eliminating our urban forests at the cost of everyone and everything else that matters. There are so many vacant and dilapidated neighborhoods that could be rehabilitated instead of destroying mature trees to build high-end homes. There seems to be little city oversight regarding the environmental effect of these projects, especially when developers sit on the planning boards. If we continue in this manner, we will have no urban forests left.

Trees act as the lungs of the Earth, keep the planet cool, help stop climate change, and provide habitat for diverse wildlife. As noted earlier, killing trees decimates entire ecosystems—living communities—teeming with plant and animal life. Even decaying trees serve as habitat to numerous critters. According to the National Wildlife Federation, more than 1,000 species of wildlife benefit from trees in various stages of decay, such as providing roosting spots for owls, bats, woodpeckers, and other creatures.

Amazing wildlife activities are taking place in our urban forests, if we take the time to look. Not long ago, I saw a small snake shedding its skin on a decaying tree stump. Snakes, of course, keep rats and mice in check. Anyone who has been on a New York City subway can tell you: "We don't want rats taking over our urban environments!" That's just one example of what happens when our ecosystems are out of balance.

We need to do more to safeguard our magnificent urban wooded areas.

PROTECTING OUR EARTH'S FORESTS

It's not just neighborhood urban trees that are being destroyed. Forests across the globe are being obliterated to make space for cattle grazing and cattle feed. I've already discussed the need to limit our beef consumption. Interestingly, my daughter's friend, who is a professional in the health field, mentioned that in her country of origin, fresh fruits are readily available and inexpensive, whereas in the United States, organic fruits and vegetables are expensive and hamburgers at fast-food chains are the inexpensive available food source that Americans consume. Not surprisingly, our health suffers when we don't eat enough fresh, healthy fruits and vegetables and instead consume food items without adequate nutrients.

Rainforests, which are essential for reducing the effects of climate change and for ensuring biodiversity, are likewise in serious trouble. Rainforests are being cleared for monoculture palm tree plantings to meet the demand for palm oil. If you do an internet search, you will discover a long list of products that contain palm oil or palm oil derivatives, which go by various names. Cleaning products, detergents, soaps, cosmetics, and shampoos are only a few of the items containing palm oil. Palm oil is also found in many processed foods and snack items like packaged chips and cookies. Because palm oil is such a big problem in deforestation, I was curious what products in my home contain palm oil. As I quickly ascertained during my inventory, a lot of common household items have palm oil. Also, don't assume that just because a product is organic or vegan, it doesn't contain palm oil.

For those of us who are fortunate to have choices regarding the products we purchase, we can opt to buy products that don't contain palm oil, or we can stop purchasing products with a high percentage of palm oil. We could also seek out products with certification that the palm oil in the product is made sustainably. In addition, we can look into companies that are exploring the use of synthetic palm oil, such as that derived from yeast fermentation. However, because palm oil use is so ubiquitous, there is no easy solution.

The more we eat locally grown foods and return to natural items for cleaning—like baking soda and vinegar —and the more we purchase goods ethically produced, the less palm oil products we will use and the less we will contribute to deforestation.

Ultimately, if it's not good for the Earth, it's not good for us.

APPRECIATING NATURE'S BEAUTY

Beautiful purple asters are blooming in my yard. Nature understands how to grow a variety of plants for each changing seasons. As I recently learned, we should not get rid of our dried native flowers in the fall or winter; the seedheads and stalks supply food for small creatures.

The birds are chatty today, with raucous blue jays and

crows calling out across the treetops. A red-bellied wood-pecker stops by, and the chipmunks and squirrels are chasing each other across the ground and around the trees. The weather is perfect and acorns are plentiful.

Somewhere high up in the tree branches, a squirrel gnaws loudly on a walnut. I suddenly spot the noisy walnut eater in the neighbor's tree; the squirrel's tail movement is visible among the leaves. The intertwined walnut trees, where the squirrel is sitting, share one base and two tall trunks. Are they one tree or two? The roots of all these neighboring trees extend below ground to the trees in my yard and interconnect in ways we can't see on the surface. As a mother, I understand the importance of connected roots within a larger community and of planting and growing in ways that benefit future offspring. Nature has so much to teach us. What an incredible world of insects, earthworms, and root systems occupy the space right below our feet! That is, assuming we have not cemented over it.

Sitting in my backyard for just a short period of time, I count four airplanes as they fly overhead, each leaving long plume trails. I wonder if somewhere there are beings who think the invention of planes and automobiles were not such great achievements after all, given what they have done to contribute to climate change and the quality of air we breathe. Was the "great" Industrial Revolution a lie taught to us in school to justify factory jobs and corporate profits? Is that what authors like Charles Dickens were trying to warn us about long ago: dirty polluting factories, corporate greed, and unhealthy working conditions, especially for the poor.

What story will we tell our great-grandchildren about our Earth? Will it be a story of how we destroyed the precious beauty of this planet and killed so many living beings with our destructive habits? Or will it be the noble tale of how we learned to care for our environment and for all creatures, great and small, who share our Earth home?

LIVING IN BALANCE AND HARMONY

The tree leaves are golden yellow—finally! They seemingly went from green to yellow overnight. Small brightly colored leaves are floating down from branches above. Moles dig below the ground, creating soft dirt in which the squirrels then bury their acorns. Some of those uneaten buried acorns will eventually grow into trees, and the cycles of Earth continue, all working in harmony—everything with a purpose that serves the greater whole, even if humans remain unaware of these life-sustaining contributions to our well-being.

I'm visiting a state park today. With so many tall trees, the leaves above create a glimmering golden canopy, with drifting leaves dancing through the air as they fall. The colorful leaves make the paths through the woods look like a magical fairyland. Similar to the falling leaves, I, too, am working on releasing and letting go at a gentle pace. A childhood where addictions, trauma, and unhealthy patterns got passed down from one generation to the next is not the path I want to follow going forward. The drama, the chaos, the verbal abuse, the violence, the justifications, and the angry outbursts—none of that helps us grow in wholesome ways. I release it all, one drifting leaf at a time.

We are capable of finding new ways.

It's not always easy to let go, even when the familiar brings unhappiness. But we must. Collectively, we have had decades of conditioning in unhealthy values—where polluting corporations and powerful men justify, or deny, the ongoing abuses toward our Earth home, putting ego, greed, and selfishness above kindness, respect, and compassion for all living things.

Can we release long-standing harmful habits, not just in our families and in our workplaces but also in relation to how we treat our Mother Earth? Can we stop justifying, making excuses, and behaving violently and, instead, recognize unhealthy actions and work toward making changes for the better? Can industry leaders who are responsible for environmental damages to our planet, and resulting harms to us, release their fierce grip on controlling, manipulating, and lying? Can we learn to treat our shared Earth home and each other with reverence and love?

In short, can we learn to live in balance and harmony on this glorious planet?

Perhaps, you are asking: What does living in balance and harmony look like? Think of it this way. If you injure your ankle, you may need to allow some time to rest your ankle in order for it to heal. If you don't let your ankle heal, you may end up doing more damage, not just to your foot but also to your hip or knees because your body is out of balance. Healing ourselves, healing our families, and healing our Earth is how we regain balance. We need to give both ourselves and our Earth home time to rest and time to heal.

Living in harmony means we understand that our being is connected to all living beings. It means living in such a way that our global human family joins in harmony with the songs of the whales, the birds, the cicadas, and the frogs. It means we begin to understand that we are part of Earth's rhythms: the ocean waves, the swaying trees, the falling rain, the twinkling night stars.

We are Earth.

As such, we know that what we do to Mother Earth, we do to ourselves.

Being in balance and harmony also means we love ourselves, we love each other, and we love Mother Earth. As the quote, attributed to Mahatma Gandhi, reminds us: "Be the change you want to see in the world." While the quote, so often repeated, may sound cliché, actually embodying that message is how we need to start living, each day, on this beautiful planet.

It means our whole being vibrates love. That is a worthy goal, indeed!

NOVEMBER RAINS

A strong breeze is blowing as a November rainstorm approaches, with leaves flying and swirling through the air like a blustery day in *Winnie-the-Pooh.*

I hear the quiet drip, drip of rain patter, and then, with a swift gush of wind, water erupts from the sky, drenching everything, while pools rapidly form on the ground. Rushing water seeks out low spots and follows paths dug out by prior rains, filling the nearby ditches. It's a heavy downpour and then, gradually, the rain becomes a quieter, steady drizzle. Soon, the heavy rains start up again.

The rain reminds me of grief. Just when we think the storm is over, it pours down even harder, once again.

Do gloomy rainy days always bring to mind worries of what's to come? Does the Earth also feel our melancholy? Do moss-covered trees and rocks weep for us? I don't know. The Earth will undoubtedly survive. But like the honey bees that pollinate the flowering plants—while also making honey that feeds the bears, raccoons, and people —aren't we humans here for a reason? And if so, what might our larger purpose be?

After the heavy rainstorms, the birds begin chirping— various pitches, songs, tweets, and trills. It is like a large family gathering over the holidays where everyone talks over everyone else while filling their bellies with food. Is it the same for birds? Are they catching up or reminiscing while filling their bellies and bathing in the puddles? So much chatter! It's hard to believe there's not some sort of celebration happening. Perhaps they're planning their trip south, catching up on news of warm air currents in faraway places, gossiping about their noisy neighbors in nearby trees, or mourning the deaths of so many of their feathered friends. Do birds mourn? Do they recognize death, loss, sorrow, and tragic misfortune? Or do they simply carry out the business of rebuilding and repairing nests after a bad storm, while eating, feeding their young, and reveling in pools of water after the rains have passed?

Hard to know. Today, they are loud. Insistent.

The sky remains gray and cloudy, but it hasn't slowed the birds' flights from branch to branch or quieted their songs. If anything, they sing much louder, now that the rains have ceased.

The Earth is nourished and life continues. Will our time here be one of celebration? Or one of mourning? What legacy will we leave for our future generations? Our great-grandchildren? Our nieces and nephews?

What will be our lasting gifts to our global family who share this earthly home?

CHAPTER EIGHT
THE NEXT GENERATION

"We can no longer let the people in power decide what is politically possible. We can no longer let the people in power decide what hope is."

— GRETA THUNBERG, ENVIRONMENTAL
ACTIVIST

STUDENT ENVIRONMENTALISM

To gather input from the younger generation on how to care for our Earth home, I am visiting Brebeuf Jesuit Preparatory School to meet with three high school students: Madison, Claire, and Ben. Like many young people who are worried about the future of our planet, these students are passionate about environmental social action.

As we sit together in the teachers' conference room, Claire and Madison discuss a grassroots, statewide student group, Confront the Climate Crisis, that tried to get a bill passed in Indiana that would establish a climate task force to study how climate change is affecting the state. As

Claire says, "The goal was to take data from research by the climate task force and create more comprehensive legislation addressing specific climate issues." While there were legislators, on both sides of the aisle, who stood by the students, disappointingly, the majority of Indiana Republican legislators were not willing to take even this most basic step of putting together a task force to study the effects of climate change—not to mention the dismal failure to exercise the leadership needed to implement proactive, policy-based climate change solutions. In fact, recent legislation actually harms our environment—such as legislation that favors the Indiana Builders Association rather than protecting wetlands.

Regardless of political inaction or setbacks, these students, as well as students across the globe, are speaking out to protect our planet and are acting on their values concerning the care of our Earth. As Claire notes, "While legislative action is definitely a portion of the solution, individual action is what is going to change it." In that vein, these students are joining with other students in ongoing, engaged environmental activism.

Ben focuses his efforts on formulating healthy habits for conservation at the school. "We put out initiatives like less trash waste, less food waste, getting more recycling bins, making those bins more accessible, and getting rid of single-use plastics." Claire adds that they are working toward the school being completely free of single-use plastic, such as using reusable water bottles and eliminating plastic cutlery. They also do trash clean-ups around the school campus.

Madison and Ben mention a thrift store run by the students and events they co-host with the fashion club to promote sustainable fashion. The conservation club also collects phone chargers and old computers to make sure those items are being recycled responsibly, and the club offers a number of ways for students to reduce their carbon footprint. Additionally, they host a speaker series where people come in to talk about specific environmental issues. The students explain that it's through conversation with others that we learn.

Madison says that in her environmental science class, their very first unit discussed climate change and how it is affecting impoverished communities. "We were all learning new things," she says. "A big problem is the lack of education about the effects of climate change. A lot of information we learned the first few months of school was shocking to most people in class. So, questions were coming up like, 'How come we didn't know about this?' and 'Why aren't more people talking about it?'" As a result, the student clubs and conservation activities are working to create change. "Sometimes there's the impression, I'm just one person, or I'm just a student and can't do anything. The clubs offer education and an opportunity to move toward actions."

Ben agrees. "We read an article in class and listened to a TED Talk about food waste and how much we're wasting. . . . It was really alarming to me and caught me off guard. Like Madison says, continuing to educate people and enlighten people is something we need to push for."

Claire stresses that more accountability is needed. Even though people have acknowledged that climate change is bad, she believes that without tangible repercussions, people fail to act. Meanwhile, those who face the biggest threats from climate change are those who live in places in the world with less money. She states, "We need to get better at empathizing with other people and also at creating systems of accountability to ensure there are tangible consequences for actions, whether that's a fine or something else. For example, if your company is doing something it shouldn't be doing, having those tangible, real-world consequences will mean accountability—that is what is going to change people's actions."

I ask the students what areas of environmental action they are most passionate about. In terms of change, Ben says, "I would like to see businesses and companies less focused on their revenues—their business model—and get outside of that to see what their larger effect on the world is." He believes that companies need to lose the idea that it's all about the money motivation, because "that is at the root of a lot of our problems."

Claire's passion centers around public green spaces. "Introducing more green spaces in metropolitan areas and in largely dense suburban areas too." She points out that a lot of lower income areas have no access to public green spaces, and that is detrimental for a lot of reasons. "The big thing for me is when children don't have anywhere to safely go when they are outside." She continues, "We build our cities and structures around a very car-centric infrastructure, and with that we reduce the amount of green space. So, when there is a park, it's four miles away, and you can only get there by car, and you'd have to cross a highway. A kid can't do that." She wants to see accessible public green spaces where kids can get outside and get fresh air and run around. "More green spaces also allow for things like community gardens and help with things like food deserts and pollution." She pauses, and then says, thoughtfully, "Who doesn't like a walkable area? It's healthier and better for the environment. If we protect those lands, then we're not using that space for buildings and factories that pollute. It's all interconnected. Preserving the land, really."

Madison's passion is sustainable fashion. She explains the environmental ills caused by society's continual need to produce and purchase fashionable, cheaply made clothing that then gets discarded. She says, "If I could wave a magic wand, I'd have a lot less fast fashion and more people shopping sustainably and knowing what impact their individual actions have."

HOW OUR CLOTHING CHOICES CAN HELP THE EARTH

Before sharing the rest of my meeting with Madison, Claire, and Ben, I want to delve for a moment into the harms of fast fashion that Madison discusses. When considering the ethical, ecological, and spiritual imperative to care for our planet, fashion apparel may not be the first thing that comes to mind. It certainly wasn't on my radar before my meeting with these high school students.

Several articles describe "fast fashion" as inexpensive trendy clothing made with synthetic fibers, such as polyester. These synthesized chemicals, known as polymers, are derived from petrochemicals, making the fashion industry heavily reliant on fossil fuels. Significantly, most of this clothing travels across the globe, produced in poor countries with textile practices that pollute the water and air while also exposing workers to dangerous chemicals.

Nowadays, the peer pressure to look good with stylish outfits occurs not only on special occasions and at public gatherings but also takes place relentlessly on the never-ending streams of social media. As the Brebeuf students explain, "In Western culture, we have an obsession with aesthetics, and the age of the internet has fed that obsession with public presentation and with everything being perfect all the time. . . . Especially when you're younger, it feels like you have to buy all these new things and fit in with the newest fashion." Fast fashion fills this desire to stay on top of chic clothing trends.

Because the clothing is cheap, people are quick to toss it aside and purchase new outfits. All this discarded clothing isn't easy to recycle due to the interwoven materials like zippers, tags, ornamentals, and buttons. According to the U.S. Environmental Protection Agency, approximately 85 percent of textiles end up in landfills—an estimated 11 million tons of textile waste annually in the United States. These synthetic fibers are not biodegradable and create harmful microfibers that threaten the land, marine life, and human health.

But some people are pushing back against fast fashion. At Brebeuf, the students started a schoolwide clothing drive for redistribution to local nonprofit organizations serving youth. Similarly for adults wanting to make a difference, there are charitable organizations that accept clothing donations for people who need job interview attire or basic clothing as a result of a domestic violence or homelessness emergency.

Sewing, knitting, or repairing our clothes is another way to avoid fast fashion. YouTube tutorials offer advice for making, repairing, and reusing clothing. If we lack such skills, we might consider taking our clothing to a professional for alterations. I saw a video on TikTok where a young woman was offering people an opportunity to mail in old clothes, and she will cut the fabric and create new clothes. When we do shop for clothes, we can go to thrift stores, buy locally, and select clothing made from organic natural fibers such as hemp.

Innovative companies also provide opportunities for people to shop sustainably. Rent the Runway, for instance, offers rental options for clothing. My youngest daughter used that service for her high school prom dress. Some companies now produce clothing using recycled materials. Nube is an example of a woman-owned company fighting climate change through sustainable activewear. Per its website, goods are made from recycled polyester and include plastic-free shipping. The outdoor clothing and gear store Patagonia, discussed more fully in the "Saving Our Planet" chapter, offers repairs for its clothing items. Other companies likewise offer repair services and/or resale options for purchased items.

These efforts toward more ecologically friendly clothing—by students and by industry leaders—signal a crucial message for us all: *We create a better world through our daily collective choices.*

MANUFACTURING HOPE

As I conclude my get-together with the Brebeuf students, I ask them about their hopes and dreams for the future. Ben says, "I want to see more people take action. I want to see more people recognizing—and getting more educated—on a lot of these topics. I want to see more out of our legislators to get climate bills through. It's a whole political money game with them. I want to see more change and then have more hope."

Madison agrees. "I am hopeful in this generation. I think there are a lot of people who want to create change. It's a matter of getting our voices heard." Claire adds, "One of the impediments to action is this nihilistic outlook that people are expressing toward climate change. With that, I just want to say, it is always better to manufacture hope for yourself so it can manifest truly. Having hope is the only way you stay motivated to be active." She says, "In the state of Indiana, I am not overly convinced that they are going to make the changes that are necessary. But on the long-term global scale with this generation accumulating more power, we are going to see an increase in climate acknowledgment, and I hope that turns to action."

Ben's advice: "Just get involved. Throw yourself into it. Deepen your values. Really focus on educating yourself. For example, care more about the ramifications of your actions. Take some time to really evaluate yourself: *How are you helping? What are you doing to make change, or what are you doing that is not supporting necessary change?*"

Claire says, "Getting involved in climate action is needed now more than ever, whether it's in your state or nation. You can find amazing groups, whether it's a group like Youth Climate Coalition, the Sierra Club, or Earth Charter. There are opportunities for you to get involved. Each voice matters and needs to be heard."

Madison concurs. "You are never just one person. It's a matter of everyone and what our collective actions do."

PART THREE
ACTION

CHAPTER NINE

SAVING OUR PLANET

"My actions are the ground upon which I stand."

— THICH NHAT HANH, BUDDHIST
MONK

BECOMING EARTH STEWARDS

I enjoy watching nature documentaries. These films often inspire a love of our Earth home. Some of them advocate for engaged environmental activism. Some offer hope amid despair. Some encourage people in affluent countries to consume less and live more closely in alignment with the rest of the world. Some highlight the need to change our food production and food consumption habits. Some documentaries reveal that if we give nature an adequate opportunity to do so, it may be able to replenish itself. As an example, prohibiting fishing in certain ocean areas for a period of time allows the previously depleted fish population to come back and to flourish. The same is true when we restore wetlands—the waterfowl, birds, fur-bearing water animals, and amphibians return to their habitat and begin to prosper.

Some documentaries give voice to the nature-based teachings of Indigenous Peoples in various parts of the world. Others bring forth faith-based or science-based appeals for urgent climate action, and some feature the voices of our youth who are calling on all of us to change directions before it's too late.

As previously mentioned, our current climate crisis won't be remedied by one magic solution. Instead, it will require our combined efforts to create a new paradigm premised on policies and actions that protect the health of our Earth and all who live here.

THE JOB OF AN ARTIST

I have been listening to a weeklong Buddhist dialogue on our climate crisis and what we should do. All in all, there is no one consensus on how to best solve our problems. Yet, the fact that so many people from various locations throughout the world care and want to help does give me hope.

Personally, I have moved from feeling overwhelmed to feeling more engaged and motivated. Even while recognizing that no one person will have all the answers, we know that one person joined with others can create a shift toward healthier ways of living on our planet. We need only do our part.

In the Buddhist online symposium, one of the speakers is an artist. He states that it is not the artist's job to offer solutions. He says to leave problem-solving for the environmentalists and the scientists because it's more important to shine a light on what is happening. I agree that shining a spotlight on social ills is critically important, and I admire science fiction writers, such as Octavia

Butler, whose doomsday scenarios sound a necessary, jarring alarm. The artist is painting a picture so people are not in denial, and the artist is raising an alarm so people will wake up! Even so, I do not feel content to leave it at simply ringing the alarm bell. I want to know: *When the alarm horn blares and the emergency sirens blast, what do we do?*

After I finish listening to the Buddhist presentations, I look outside my office window and see a brown squirrel stretched out on the tree branch, taking a nap. I observe how the squirrel blends in perfectly with its surroundings; it looks like a nodule on the tree with brown fur that is almost indistinguishable from the bark. Blending in well to our environment can mean survival. Being invisible to predators helps ensure our continued existence. But it's not the job of an artist to be invisible. An artist takes risks, gives voice, and sometimes stands out. It can be a scary prospect, especially in my case when standing out in an alcoholic home as a child could mean physical harm. Standing out can be dangerous. Normally, I prefer to avoid it at all costs!

Only, I am an adult now, not a child at the mercy of others. And I love the deep peace found in forests, and I love wildflowers, waterfalls, and birds. I love nature *more* than I fear the opinions of others. What will happen to Mother Earth if we do not take care of her? What will happen to the wildlife we love? What will happen to us if our water, food, land, and air become sick with poisons? How do we get healthy?

I recall a family of deer I saw walking in my neighborhood during the COVID-19 pandemic and how few cars were on the roads during the lockdowns. That period gave us a small glimpse of blue skies, less traffic noise, and fewer airplane plumes. It showed us how connected we are in times of a global health crisis.

We cannot continue with business as usual if we desire

a sustainable, healthy life. All the money, power, and riches will not save us from diseases and from environmental catastrophes such as floods, droughts, hurricanes, and intense wildfires. When we are out of balance, *every living being suffers*. We must heal. We must learn. We must dare to change.

Lastly, we must find a way to return home to our hearts, to our global family, and to our Mother Earth. We must listen to the birds, the wind, the river, and the piercing cry of an eagle soaring above.

We must begin to care. And we must begin to act.

MINDFUL LIVING

When wondering how to take care of our Earth home, becoming more mindful of our daily actions is a beneficial place to begin. We can pay attention, each day, to what we eat, what we purchase, what we wear, how we travel, how we construct and heat or cool our buildings, how we govern our cities, states and nations, how we grow our food, how we run our businesses, how we care for people who are less fortunate, and what we teach our young people. Essentially, how we live—*our daily choices*—directly affects the health and well-being of this fragile ecosystem in which we dwell, as well as the health of all living beings with whom we share this space.

For anyone wanting to do more or learn more, one useful action we can take is to support the community leaders—and organizations—who are already diligently working to ensure that our Earth home is healthy, whether it's caring for our urban spaces, farmlands, oceans, forests, mountains, lakes, rivers, streams, prairies, wetlands, soil, food, wildlife, or the air we breathe. We can also elect government representatives whose actions demonstrate a commitment to protecting our environment and the health of future generations.

Finally, we can put together an Earth Sustainability Action Plan for our workplaces, nonprofit organizations, businesses, places of worship, governments, homes, schools, cities, and nations, all across the world. (See the chapter on "Earth Sustainability Circles" for more on this topic.)

Now, the present moment, is where we begin our personal and collective shift toward healthy living on a healthy planet.

A FEW WORDS ABOUT PLASTICS

Did you know that most conventional plastic comes from fossil fuels? According to EcoJustice, Canada's largest environmental law charity, the vast majority of plastics are made from oil and gas, "with more than 99 percent made from chemicals sourced from fossil fuels." Moreover, per an article in *Ecowatch* by scientist David Suzuki, quoting the Center for International Environmental Law staff attorney Steven Feit, "'Fossil fuels and plastics are not only made from the same materials, they are made by the same companies. Exxon is both the gas in your car and the plastic in your water bottle.'" As Suzuki emphasizes, "The best way to avoid the massive damage that comes with plastics and fossil fuels is to stop using so many."

While walking over a bridge after a recent storm, I glance down and notice a large amount of plastic garbage amassed in the stream below. I've also seen piles of plastic water bottles and other such trash accumulated on beaches, in roadside ditches, and in riverbeds. High-end hotels frequently give out plastic water bottles to guests, adding to the problem. Work conferences and event venues in the United States may also supply plastic water bottles to the people in attendance. With over 300 million tons of plastic produced each year—and some organizations estimate that number may double in the next thirty years— our plastic use is causing serious environmental problems.

How many vending machines, gas station stores, grocery stores, entertainment and sports arenas sell plastic water bottles and plastic beverage bottles? How much revenue are these companies generating? How much garbage are we creating? On top of that, we have plastic packaging and other single-use plastic products that routinely get tossed aside.

According to Ocean Conservancy, an international organization working to protect our oceans, many of the plastics we use in our daily lives are used once and then thrown out, and much of this plastic ends up in our oceans, affecting nearly 700 species. Its website indicates that "plastic has been found in more than 60% of all seabirds and in 100% of sea turtle species that mistake plastic for food." Significantly, the Nature Conservancy has found, "About 11 million tons of plastic enters the ocean every year. . . . But plastic isn't just in the ocean, it's everywhere. It's in our drinking water, it falls in our rain, and studies show that harmful plastic pollution disproportionately affects disadvantaged communities. No matter who you are, or where you live, plastic is in your body."

Per Oceana, an organization focused on ocean conservation, recycling programs do not solve the problems of our plastic pollution. It states that chemical recycling exacerbates the climate crisis. Citing Global Alliance for Incinerator Alternatives, "plastic-to-fuel facilities release toxic chemicals into the air and overburden low-income communities and communities of color." Oceana says, "The only way to reduce the amount of material we landfill or incinerate is to reduce the amount we produce in the first place," which supports the statement by scientist David Suzuki that less plastic consumption is the best solution for avoiding the massive harms that result from our use of plastics and fossil fuels.

Fortunately, some beach resorts have started banning single-use plastic because of the damage to sea life. Environmentally responsible hotels are now offering guests reusable water bottles. In the United States, a few states have also begun to ban or restrict single-use plastics. For example, single-use plastic bans or restrictions have been adopted in California, Connecticut, Delaware, Hawaii, Maine, New York, and Vermont. Visit The Nature Conservancy's website for information regarding California's comprehensive and ambitious policy to reduce pollution from single-use plastics. Schools are making strides in banning single-use plastics as well.

One simple action we can take is to contact the places we frequent—such as our workout facilities, museums, schools, hospitals, park visitor centers, and workplaces—to request the removal of single-use plastics, including vending machines selling beverages in plastic bottles. Better to sell a reusable water container than continuing to contribute to pollution from single-use plastic bottles that get tossed aside. The same suggestion applies to people of influence, such as celebrities in sports and entertainment who are endorsing beverages in plastic bottles or hosting large venue events with a lot of plastic garbage.

Finally, we can make choices as consumers not to purchase single-use plastic products, and we can contact our government representatives to advocate for actions that curb ongoing plastic pollution.

LIVING OUR VALUES

During the course of writing this book, people have mentioned to me various advances being made in certain areas of environmental concern, such as innovative efforts toward eradicating plastic pollution, sometimes with a dismissive tone that implies we don't *really* need to worry about these issues. It may be that the environmental harms mentioned in this book will be remedied over time —that is the hope! But it will not solve our problems if we make progress in one area, only to continue along destructive paths that disregard the ongoing care of our Earth home.

To illustrate this point, I will share a brief example. A few years ago, while on vacation with my family at a very nice beach resort, I was sitting at a table having lunch in an outdoor courtyard. I glanced over at a nearby table as five teenagers got up and walked away, leaving all their food wrappers and trash on the table. I stood up and hurried over to the departing group, yelling, "Excuse me!" They turned around, and I said, "You left all your garbage on the table." One young woman looked at me and said, "Oh, sorry," as she headed back to clear off the mess on the table. The other individuals, three young men and one woman, continued their conversation, ignoring me as they walked away without glancing back.

Perhaps you have witnessed similar behavior, where someone throws trash out of a car window or leaves heaps of trash to accumulate on our roadways, in our neighborhoods, in the alleys, in the lakes, rivers, and oceans, and on the beaches. If we have total indifference for the messes we are creating, then we have lost our way. Our technological environmental advances aren't going to save us from ourselves.

When I was in Europe visiting my daughter, the young

man she is dating asked me, "Is it true about all the red plastic cups in American?" His question did not make any sense to me. I replied, "What red plastic cups?" He continued, "In the movies, everyone at parties has alcohol drinks in red plastic cups, and they also play drinking games using plastic cups." I realized he was talking about Hollywood movies that show people partying at a college frat house, at a beach bonfire, or at a fancy house with a pool. I pondered his question for a minute. *Is it true about all the red plastic cups?* I answered, "Yes, I think so. I guess I never noticed." Now, when I watch a movie or television program that has a drinking scene, I notice all the red plastic cups, and I see what he saw as an observer from another country.

In real life, the plastic cups at parties likely end up in plastic trash bags or are left as litter. Something that was not previously on my radar is now obvious. That may be the case for most of us. We have something brought to our attention, and then we begin to notice it more often.

If we want to make real progress in the care of our Earth home, we will need to bring to our full attention the environmental problems we have failed to address—*or even notice*—as well as the actions necessary to remedy these harms.

We may also need to look more closely at our values. Do our values include caring for our Earth? Do our values include not polluting? Do our values include putting people, wildlife, and nature ahead of profits? Do our values include honesty from corporate leaders and government representatives about the environmental harms caused by the burning of fossil fuels and by industrial pollutants. Do our values include making sure that all communities are regarded equally? Do our values include working with diverse groups of people, rather than sowing dissension? Do our values include supporting

188 DIANA J. ENSIGN, J.D.

those civic leaders who are working to safeguard our planet?

In the earlier example I shared where the youth left their garbage sitting on the table, if I had asked them—or their parents—about their values, they may have said, "Of course we care about our Earth!" But how do we move from glib answers about our values to actually *living* these values in our daily actions and through our collective choices? Are we teaching young people to care about the right things? Is caring for our Earth home a high priority in our families, in our schools, in our places of worship, in our government, and in our culture?

What do we need to do differently to instill a strong, ongoing commitment for the care of Mother Earth?

ADOPTING A CIRCULAR ECONOMY

An additional approach to reducing greenhouse gas emissions—as well as working to reduce landscape and habitat destruction—is practicing what is known as a circular economy. Rather than consuming goods and then just throwing them away, the principles of a circular economy involve sharing, reusing, leasing, repairing, refurbishing, and recycling goods, such as our clothing mentioned earlier. The circular economy also involves making more durable, efficient, and sustainable products right from the start in order to reduce energy and resource consumption.

The Ellen MacArthur Foundation—a charity committed to creating a global circular economy—states that the main pillars of a circular economy are to eliminate waste and pollution, circulate products and materials, and regenerate nature. According to an article in the World Resources Institute, "As circular economy strategies reduce the demand for raw materials and new products, they can help reduce global emissions from half the global total that come from the extraction and processing of materials." Examples of key focus areas for reducing emissions include buildings and construction, food systems, and plastics.

Europe is leading the way on the circular economy movement with the European Union's Circular Economy Action Plan put into place as part of the Green Deal. According to an article in *Sustainability* magazine, the Netherlands, France, and Italy are taking bold steps to make the circular economy a reality. The former Prime Minister of the Netherlands approved plans and specific projects that aim for transition to a 100 percent circular economy by 2050. France likewise enacted legislation and several projects promoting a circular economy, such as making it mandatory for supermarkets to give away unsold food to charities and thereby help to reduce food waste. Italy also has adopted projects that work toward sustainability, a circular economy, and climate change mitigation. Numerous other countries, such as the United Kingdom, Spain, Germany, Finland, and Belgium, to name only a few, are making progress toward a circular economy as well. The Circular Economy Network notes that countries across the globe, such as China and Japan, have implemented practices to reduce waste through a circular economy.

Innovators and entrepreneurs everywhere are finding ways in their communities to contribute toward a circular economy through repair programs, recycling programs, fashion and food waste programs, plastic packaging prohibitions, refurbishing and/or repair options for electronic goods, and so on. Zero waste is a commendable goal when it comes to consumer goods and the health of our planet.

BETTER BUSINESS MODELS

Earth sustainability efforts entail more than listing a few green initiative goals on a company website. A better model for conducting business in a sustainable way involves implementing Earth stewardship practices throughout *all* business operations.

This eco-friendly approach requires an evaluation of a company's carbon footprint and an ongoing analysis of how the entire business operation can be improved to align with Earth-friendly values. As consumers, it's impor-tant to look beyond vague statements to ensure a company is not "greenwashing" (i.e., using words that sound good but do not demonstrate concrete, verifiable changes in business practices). We can also support those businesses that do align with our Earth values.

Patagonia, an outdoor clothing and gear store, received the United Nations Champions of the Earth award for its efforts toward sustainability in the retail busi-ness. Aiming for slow fashion, the company website indi-cates that Patagonia uses recycled materials in 87 percent of its products and offers clothing repair options. It is at 100 percent renewable electricity in the United States and 76 percent globally. Notably, 1 percent of sales are pledged to the preservation and restoration of the natural environ-ment. Patagonia also contributes to over 1,000 environ-mental organizations.

More recently, the company transferred ownership to a trust that seeks to combat climate change and protect nature. According to Patagonia founder Yvon Chouinard, the company is purpose-driven: fighting the environmental crisis, defending nature, and working to save the planet. Per Patagonia, Earth stewardship is integrated into every aspect of its business operations, and it is transparent about its business practices. As stated in its mission: "We're in business to save our home planet."

Patagonia is an example of a business working to address its environmental impact. Yet, even with its laudable Earth-friendly initiatives—which are *far above* many companies—there still remain areas for improvement. For instance, according to *Follow the Money*, an investigative journalism platform in the Netherlands, Patagonia's supply chain includes foreign factories that are not paying their workers a living wage. Patagonia's website is transparent about this issue and points to its ongoing efforts for attaining living wages in these factories. Whether this serious problem is eventually resolved remains to be seen.

While no business undertaking is perfect, the goal is to evolve in our understanding and in our methods to ensure that our *actions*—whether as producers or as consumers—match our values. Assessing the environmental effect of business operations—throughout the entire supply chain—and making changes accordingly is a useful place to begin.

As already discussed in the section on fast fashion, "How Our Clothing Choices Can Help the Earth," consuming less, repairing older clothing, shopping locally from thrift stores, and purchasing durable goods made from organic natural fibers are potential solutions for fast fashion's waste and pollution problems. Supporting businesses that are making strides toward Earth-friendly measures—not just in clothing retail but in all consumer sectors—is another way we can influence positive change. We can also ask questions and hold companies accountable when they fail to protect our planet and all who live here.

As we move toward healthy Earth practices in our professional activities, we raise the bar for others to do better. We also demonstrate what is possible in our business models as we adjust our methods of doing business.

B CORPORATIONS AND BOOK PUBLISHING

As individuals who care about our Earth home, sometimes we recognize that while things are not exactly as we would like them to be, or as they SHOULD be, we are doing the best we can with the options available to us. The reality is that industry leaders must make the necessary environmental changes to address climate change, as well as hazardous pollution. And we need to advocate for those changes!

Per the U.S. Environmental Protection Agency (EPA), the main human activity that accounts for over 70 percent of all United States greenhouse gas emissions is the combustion of fossil fuels (**coal, natural gas, and oil**) for energy and transportation. Many industrial processes also emit carbon dioxide through fossil fuel consumption. As earlier chapters pointed out, that is a top concern! The EPA states, "The most effective way to reduce CO_2 emissions is to reduce fossil fuel consumption." Climate scientist Katharine Hayhoe agrees. "We need collective action and that means changing the system."

While individual action alone will not solve our environmental challenges, there are ways in which we can contribute toward Earth-friendly choices—some of which have already been discussed. Because I believe in "walking the talk," it is worth mentioning my process for publishing this book. First, I reflected on what I needed to know in order to move my consumerism in a sustainable direction. In seeking out book publishers, I asked: Does this printing/publishing company have sustainability practices? Is the organization looking at paper usage, clean energy, and environmental justice?

Unfortunately, the majority of book publisher websites I explored did not contain any sustainability information. Nevertheless, we each have a voice, and we can use it to speak up for the Earth. So, I wanted to at least email potential publishers to ask: "Do you have an environmental sustainability statement that explains what measures you are taking to protect the planet as you operate your business?"

Sometimes, my query was ignored. Sometimes, the reply was that the publisher did not have an environmental sustainability statement, which was especially surprising because most of the companies I looked at were known for publishing books about spirituality and the environment. A few publishers I contacted are actively taking measures to publish in a sustainable way, either through their business practices or through a parent publishing company. But as I have learned, various factors go into a book publisher's decision-making process regarding whom they take on as an author.

As you might guess, unless you're already famous and can sell millions of books, writers don't get to decide who will publish their book—even if the publishing company has beneficial Earth stewardship practices. One smaller publishing company, for instance, told me that it could not take on my book project right now because it is having trouble competing with the large publishing houses. Other factors—such as a pandemic, embargoes, or fires—can affect paper availability, production costs, and a publisher's backlog (i.e., inability to take on additional book projects).

My books are published through my imprint, Spirit-Hawk Life Publications. Traditional publishers I contacted have not been willing to take me on as a writer who cannot guarantee them large revenues. Consequently, my books have been self-published print-on-demand, meaning copies are printed as they are ordered, reducing paper

waste and requiring less need for transportation and stor-
age. Because print-on-demand books are not mass
produced, it also means less excess inventory that ends up
in landfills.

As an additional eco-friendly measure, I support
nonprofit organizations through financial contributions,
including donations to The Nature Conservancy (global
environmental organization), The Lambi Fund of Haiti
(working on reforesting efforts in Haiti), Bat Conservation
International (global conservation organization dedicated
to ending bat extinctions), Friends of Goose Pond (supports wildlife conservation and habitat restoration at
Goose Pond Fish and Wildlife Area in Greene County
Indiana), and Sycamore Land Trust (conservation organization protecting land and restoring habitat in southern
Indiana).

For this book, copies that are bought through my
website or at my speaking events are printed by Lulu
Press, which not only prints books on demand but also
uses paper certified by the Forest Stewardship Council
(FSC). That means the product comes from forests that
are managed with strict, high environmental standards
that ensure biodiversity. FSC-certified paper is a sustainable and ethical choice. Although it took quite a lot of
work to find a press that uses FSC-certified paper, I was
thrilled to discover that Lulu meets this standard. If you
purchased this book via Amazon, it is unknown what
sustainability measures are followed. Of course, if you
purchased this book as an eBook, sustainable paper is not
part of the equation.

People may assume that authors are rich. Actually, so
far, I have considered myself lucky if I break even (and
that does not take into account my time spent writing,
which is typically two years or more). Additional printing
costs might mean the difference between breaking even

and taking a big financial loss, though I hope that is not the case. My point is that such decisions are not easy and not financially feasible for everyone. That is why we need industries to make the needed changes. An individual is not always in the best position to do so.

Another important factor that went into my decision to use Lulu Press for printing my book copies is that the company is a Certified B Corporation. What does that mean?

In short, B Lab is a global nonprofit organization that sets B Corporation (B Corp) standards for a company's social and environmental performance. B Corp certification requires accountability, transparency, and an assessment of its methods—such as how it treats its employees, its charitable giving, its environmental practices, and so on. Per the B Lab website, its mission is to "transform the economic system into a more inclusive, equitable, and regenerative economy." Lulu Press satisfies the B Corp certification criteria through 100 percent renewable energy consumption, paid volunteer days for employees, and in-office composting and gardening, along with other sustainable practices.

There are over 7,000 certified B Corps in various locations around the globe. Many of these companies are engaged in social justice activism and Earth-friendly measures, such as supporting regenerative agriculture, using responsible sourced packaging, and speaking out for climate change solutions.

Whatever our profession or our roles in life, asking questions about an organization's sustainability practices is a good way to make eco-friendly choices—and may get the ball rolling for organizational leaders who have not yet tackled pressing climate change issues in their business operations. Progress may take time. It may require persistence. It almost certainly will not happen overnight. Yet we can give our best efforts toward making a positive difference. We can also do so more effectively by uniting our collective voices in this ongoing, critical work. (See upcoming chapter on "Forming Earth Sustainability Circles.")

Saving our planet is about integrating the care of our Earth into *everything* we do, as best as we are able to. Together, I believe we will find our way.

OUR LASTING LEGACY

To wrap up my yearlong environmental exploration—which ended up being over two years—I am visiting Goose Pond Fish & Wildlife Area in Greene County, Indiana, for its annual Marsh Madness Festival. This festival highlights the migration of sandhill cranes, whooping cranes, and innumerable waterfowl to a 9,000-acre marsh/prairie habitat.

The Marsh Madness Festival is hosted by Friends of Goose Pond, a community-based nonprofit, and takes place each year in late February. It is a celebration of a magnificent natural area that instills a strong conservation ethic through a variety of cultural, educational, and wildlife experiences for individuals, families, and children.

I am sharing my visit to Goose Pond because even though everyone is happily enjoying the festival activities today, initially the local residents voiced strong objections to this large-scale wetland restoration project. Now, over a decade later, Goose Pond is celebrated for providing quality outdoor recreational opportunities with an estimated 12,000 visits each year from birders and wildlife watchers! Like many big undertakings, this wetland project came about through partnerships, including the combined efforts of the USDA Natural Resources Conservation Service, The Nature Conservancy, U.S. Fish &

Wildlife Service, and other environmental and wildlife organizations.

At present, Goose Pond is one of the largest wetland restorations in the United States, with more than 260 bird species recorded, including tens of thousands of sandhill cranes, American white pelicans, and snow geese that sometimes number over 100,000! The birds and other wildlife make their home on thousands of acres of diverse wetlands, new tree plantings, and native prairie restorations.

As I join the other guests at the Goose Pond Visitor Center for this annual commemorative event, I notice a handful of people gathered outside the building. The weather is sunny and breezy, making it a pleasant day for visitors. When I head outdoors, a man quietly calls me over to his telescope, where he directs my gaze to an eagle perched high in a tree across the water. I lean over, peering through the telescope lens, and then spot this miraculous raptor in all its glory! An eagle is a thrilling sight to behold.

Later, back inside the Visitor Center for the official gala, I watch a group of young children giggling as they scamper about looking at the informative wildlife displays. Always, children bring hope for the future, motivating us to protect and preserve our Earth home. After remarks from community leaders, everyone goes outside for a brief hike. We then head over to an area where people are observing sandhill cranes, pelicans, ducks, and whooping cranes.

This wonderful nature preserve holds a special place in my heart because my husband, while working as state biologist for the federal Natural Resources Conservation Service, is one of the people who early on faced heated opposition from local residents during the Goose Pond restoration work. He is alive today to see it come full circle as a celebrated achievement! Not all of us are fortunate enough to see the benefits of the work we do during our lifetime. On the contrary, innumerable people throughout history never saw the fruits of their labor when striving to advance humanity toward a more compassionate, just, and loving world.

For the individuals who steadfastly worked to restore Goose Pond—and for the people who continue the work of preserving and maintaining our natural areas—it is a labor of love. These people who dedicated decades to this wetland restoration project have said that Goose Pond is their legacy—a legacy that will still be here after they are gone; a legacy passed on to benefit wildlife, their community, and future generations.

Goose Pond is an amazing testament to what is possible with hard work, community partnerships, and a shared vision. It is just one example of *so many* such efforts across the planet by people working to preserve and safeguard our exquisite Earth home. I bow in deep gratitude to these tenacious and heroic humans. Thank you!

Glancing toward the sky, I see a huge flock of whooping cranes taking flight over the glistening water.

May we all hold fast to the beautiful possibilities before us.

CHAPTER TEN

FORMING EARTH SUSTAINABILITY CIRCLES

"Never doubt that a small group of thoughtful, committed citizens
can change the world; indeed, it's the only thing that ever has."

— MARGARET MEAD,
ANTHROPOLOGIST

CREATING HEALTHY COMMUNITIES

There's a famous quote, "Blessed are those who plant trees under whose shade they will never sit." We plant trees for our children, our grandchildren, and our great-grandchildren. We plant trees for our Earth home. We plant trees for the benefit of all living beings.

In other words, the future depends on what we do today.

Creating healthy communities will require ALL of us to be actively engaged—in a variety of capacities—in the ongoing, collective efforts to safeguard our planet. With that shared purpose in mind, we can strive to learn from one another and work together for a common goal. Know that we can change the world for the better.

One way to begin the process of caring for our Earth is by forming Earth Sustainability Circles. If you already have a green team or creation care committee, consider expanding that group wider—perhaps out into the community—with a newly formed Earth Sustainability Circle. For instance, if you have a stewardship green team at your place of worship, you might consider an interfaith Earth Sustainability Circle to learn what others are doing and to share useful information.

In our Earth Sustainability Circles, we can continue to address the questions raised at the beginning of this book:

- *What harmful human actions are causing our environmental crisis?*
- *How do we learn to work together to solve the challenges we face?*
- *What positive actions can we take to benefit our Earth home and all of Earth's inhabitants?*

More importantly, as we join together to answer these questions—along with whatever new questions come up during our Earth-care explorations—we will advance our collective knowledge regarding potential solutions.

We can then put these remedies into policies and practices in our communities.

BEGIN TODAY

Start your own Earth Sustainability Circle. Invite a group of neighbors, parents, coworkers, book club members, friends, or people from your place of worship to join you. That's how we make significant change—not alone but in community with people who care and with people who take action to create a better world for everyone.

We don't have to feel helpless or isolated. Even a small

group of individuals who gather once a month can provide sustaining, mutual support for the work ahead. It is both motivating and inspiring to be with people who share our values.

The Earth Sustainability Circles are divided into ten sessions, focusing each time on a different environmental topic. These sessions explore the challenges, potential solutions, and action plan ideas. Action steps can then be implemented in your household, school, local business, nonprofit organization, place of worship, city, state, or nation. But before we get to the discussion topics, I want to go over a few preliminary items.

SET YOUR INTENTIONS

When you form your Earth Sustainability Circle, here are a few questions to consider as you frame your intentions for the group:

- **Earth Sustainability Circle Participants.** What type of circle gathering do you want to create? For instance, will the group be a sacred circle, with opening/closing readings, rituals, and candle lightings? Will the meetings be grounded in faith-based or spiritual-based values? Or will the gatherings be purely social with friends and neighbors? Or will the gatherings be offered as part of a professional group or organization?
- **Open or Closed.** Will the Earth Sustainability Circle gatherings be open to the general public or will they be limited in size and offered by invitation only?
- **Size of the Group.** How many people do you want joining the circle? Will youth be

invited? What about marginalized members of your community? How will you reach out to the people you wish to invite?

- **Frequency of Meetings.** How often will the circle meet: once a week, semimonthly, or once a month? How many meetings will you have? The Earth Sustainability Circle discussion topics are set up for ten initial meetings.
- **Location.** What location will be used for the Earth Sustainability Circle gatherings? Will the meeting place rotate or stay in one location?
- **Length**. How long will the meetings last? Will there be food or refreshments and, if so, are there ways to do so without plasticware? Is child care needed?
- **Expanded Circles.** If you are already part of a green team or creation care committee, how might these gatherings extend beyond the walls of your organization? How might you create or host Earth Sustainability Circles for your local community?
- **Purpose.** What is the overall goal of the Earth Sustainability Circle? The purpose and mission of the circle could be something that is discussed at the first gathering.

HOW TO ENGAGE ON TOUGH SUBJECTS

Not everyone who joins together for an Earth Sustainability Circle is going to agree on how best to handle our environmental challenges—even when the vision and mission of the group align with the values of the people who attend. Some topics are triggering or upsetting for us, depending on our backgrounds, beliefs, experiences, and attitudes. We don't have to reach an agreement during the circle gatherings. Simply engaging in honest dialogue can be a useful starting place. But we do need to remain respectful.

In that regard, it may be necessary to establish a few ground rules for the group. Consider sharing the following guidelines with your Earth Sustainability Circle at the onset:

1. Listen with an open mind and an open heart.
2. Speak from the heart and from personal experience using "I" statements.
3. Approach the conversations with curiosity. Lifelong learning, which includes making mistakes, is a worthwhile and brave undertaking. We all have something to contribute with our presence, and no one is an expert on everything.
4. Fully listen to what the other person is saying rather than listening simply to reply.
5. Decide ahead of time if the group conversations are going to remain confidential.
6. Accept people where they are. Try not to judge yourself or others.
7. Be respectful. No yelling, name-calling, belittling, or gossiping.
8. Avoid cross-talk, that is, interrupting or talking over someone who is speaking.
9. Be kind to one another.
10. Find shared values, even if you disagree on a difficult topic or specific solution. A valuable intention for the circle might be connection and community building, ahead of actions.
11. Breathe. Allow space for quiet reflection.
12. End the circle gathering with gratitude.

TEN DISCUSSION SESSIONS

As noted, the Earth Sustainability Circles are divided into ten sessions with prompts for taking action steps. Each meeting will begin with a check-in and conclude with dialogue regarding possible action steps before the next gathering.

These Earth Sustainability Circles are a starting point. Your gatherings may end up going beyond the initial ten sessions. The circle group might, for instance, decide to spend additional time diving more deeply into one environmental focus area. Or the group may want to continue meeting socially for outings to visit vegan restaurants, organic farms, or nature preserves. Or the group might want to host speakers on ecological topics of interest. In whatever way the Earth Sustainability Circle evolves, may the seeds we plant through our combined actions grow to create healthy, loving communities.

In the next chapter, we will explore book topics for discussion and ask questions intended to spark ideas for implementing Earth-friendly actions. With respect to the action steps, you can always do more than the suggested number of action steps. You can also do less or none at all if you don't have the time or energy at present. Sometimes, just being with like-minded people is enough. The action step discussions may prompt you to revisit a point of interest at a future date. Also, hearing what others are doing can inspire us. Remember, learning from one another in community counts as an enormously valuable action step throughout this process!

In closing, I want to thank each of you for your commitment to this mission of collectively caring for our Earth home! The trees, oceans, plants, birds, and animals undoubtedly extend their gratitude as well!

CHAPTER ELEVEN

EARTH SUSTAINABILITY CIRCLE DISCUSSION TOPICS

SESSION ONE: INTRODUCTIONS

INTRODUCE YOURSELF: Welcome to the Earth Sustainability Circle. Take a few moments to introduce yourself to the group. What motivated you to join an Earth Sustainability Circle? What are you hoping to gain through this book discussion and group process? What are your hopes for the Circle?

CHECK-IN. Do you ever feel overwhelmed or stressed by the news of our environmental problems? What helps you feel less overwhelmed?

The author begins this book by expressing her feelings of being overwhelmed by the magnitude of our environmental challenges and the climate crises we are facing. Believing we are helpless can lead to despair, whereas taking one small step or making a decision to act can help move us forward in positive ways. In the book, the author went on a nature retreat and set her intention to explore environmental topics for one year. In this session, we will examine what intentions

*we wish to set for our Earth Sustainability Circle and what we might
need in terms of self-care.*

Questions to Explore

1. EARTH CARE. What, if any, personal or professional
activities are you currently involved in regarding the stewardship of our Earth home?

2. SELF-CARE. Do you find time for self-care and quiet
reflection? Do you keep a journal, meditate, or practice
some form of relaxation on a regular basis? What are the
additional ways you could practice more self-care? How
might caring for our Earth and caring for our personal
well-being be connected?

3. RESPECT. Do you think there's a link between
violence against women—and violence against Indigenous
Peoples, Blacks, LGBTQ individuals, and other marginalized groups—and the violence we are witnessing against
Mother Earth? How can we better teach respect and
model reverence for all inhabitants of our Earth home?

4. TOP THREE CONCERNS. What issues are closest
to your heart when it comes to taking care of our Earth
home? Make a list of the top three items of concern for
our planet and/or for the living beings here on Mother
Earth. If you could wave a magic wand, what would you
most like to see improved or changed regarding the stewardship of our Earth home?

1. _____

2. _____

3. _____

5. MISSION STATEMENT. Write out a mission statement that reflects your pledge (or goals) for the Earth Sustainability Circle, such as: I/We commit to showing up and listening with an open heart and mind.

During our meetings over the next ten sessions, my intention—or the intention for our group—is as follows:
_____ and
_____.

ACTION STEP: What is one action you can take before the next Earth Sustainability Circle gathering to address an environmental issue you care about? Perhaps there is something you can do for your own self-care? Perhaps your action step is learning more about an environmental topic or making a plan to spend a few hours in nature? Be specific.

———

SESSION TWO: OUR NEIGHBORHOOD LANDSCAPES

CHECK-IN: If you engaged in an action step after the last session, how did it go? Share if you learned anything from that experience?

According to the author, our well-being and the well-being of the planet depend upon fostering a healthy, diverse native plant community. This section will take a look at how we might create more Earth-friendly landscapes in our local areas.

Questions to Explore

1. DESCRIBE YOUR LOCAL ENVIRONMENT.
What is the landscape like where you live? For instance, do you live in a city, rural area, suburban neighborhood, or on farmland? Are there trees? Are there native plants and organic gardens? Are there adequate green spaces? Do you live near water? Are there polluting factories, or other pollutants, in your local environment?

2. COMMUNITY LANDSCAPES. What is the landscape like where you work, frequently visit, or attend school? What about the environment beyond your local neighborhood? What is the landscape like in your larger area, such as a nearby city or town? What about the landscape of your state/province or region; what is it like? What about in your country? How is the overall environment in terms of green spaces, pollution, trees, organic gardens, and so on?

3. NATIVE PLANTS. Are you familiar with plants that are native to your area and those that are invasive? Does your residence, neighborhood, school, workplace, or place of worship have native pollinator plants? Is there enough diversity and quantity of native vegetation to provide habitat for animal, bird, and insect species? Are there spaces in your local region that could be converted into native plant areas or green spaces for the community?

4. PRAIRIES AND WETLANDS. Are there adequate wetlands and prairies in your community that reduce water runoff and increase groundwater infiltration? Is the land in your business and residential areas composed primarily of non-native grasses, cement, or roads?

5. ENVIRONMENTAL TOXINS. Is your landscape healthy and free of toxins? Have you noticed any problems related to how the natural environment is being treated? Are insecticides, herbicides, and other pesticides indiscriminately used for lawn care, landscaping, and/or farming? Are the parks in your area utilizing native plants and avoiding chemical sprays?

6. RESOURCES. Do you have any native seed/plant nurseries in your area? Which nonprofit organizations, government resources, or university experts could you enlist for community education about the benefits of native plants, the harms of invasive plants, and the dangers of chemical pesticides? Perhaps someone working for the parks, schools, local government, or an environmental nonprofit group has a passion for sharing native plant information? Is there a native plant society in your community?

ACTION STEPS: What two actions can you take before the next Earth Sustainability Circle gathering to address an environmental issue where you live, work, worship, or attend school? How might the landscape in your local

community—or in your state, province/region, or country
—be improved? Is there an action step that might improve
the landscape of the areas alongside roadways, businesses,
schools, and places of worship? Is there someone in a
leadership position that you could contact to learn more?

———

SESSION THREE: OUR FOOD CONSUMPTION

CHECK-IN: How did your action step(s) from last time go? Share if you learned anything from that experience. How are you feeling about our collective Earth care?

Our well-being and the well-being of the planet is affected by how we produce our food—such as the use of chemicals and artificial fertilizers and the distance from production to consumption, or the carbon footprint—and also by what we eat, such as beef from large-scale factory farms versus organic plant-based food options available to us.

Questions to Explore

1. WHERE DOES YOUR FOOD COME FROM?
From where do you get the majority of the food that you or your family consume? Is your food nutritious? Is the soil where your food is grown free from pesticides? Is your food organic? Is it local? Do you eat a lot of highly processed foods?

2. HEALTHY EATING OPTIONS. Do you have
access to organic fresh vegetables and fruits for your daily meals? Are there community gardens in your neighborhood? What about food co-ops? Are there any farmers' markets near you? Do cafeterias in your workplace, schools, and hospitals offer nutritious, organic, plant-based food options? What about nearby restaurants: are there affordable organic, plant-based food items on the menu?

3. FOOD ACCESS. Are there ways to ensure that
marginalized communities and impoverished people in your region have access to free organic produce, perhaps grown in urban gardens, hoop houses, and/or green roof

gardens? Are there grant opportunities, nonprofit organizations, places of worship, or government incentives that can assist with starting a local organic community garden or food co-op?

4. BEEF CONSUMPTION. How much beef do you consume weekly or monthly? Have you explored eating less beef, such as adopting the Meatless Mondays plant-based program or eating at a vegetarian or vegan restaurant? Have you experimented with plant-based recipes or tried eating meals with lentils, chickpeas, or black beans instead of beef?

5. HEALTHY MEALS. Do you cook homemade meals? How often do you consume prepackaged, highly processed fast food? Are there ways for you to eat healthier, such as snacking on nuts or sliced fruit instead of chips or by making a pot of healthy soup? What changes might be doable for you or for your family in this regard?

ACTION STEPS: What action step can you take for healthier eating? For example, if we stop buying items such as corn chips or ice cream, we might be less tempted to snack on unhealthy food in the evenings. Perhaps you can organize a group outing to a vegetarian or vegan restaurant or host a healthy food plant-based pitch-in, maybe for the final Earth Sustainability Circle gathering? Or you might want to advocate for nutritious lunches in a school, work setting, or hospital cafeteria? Or perhaps you can explore joining, or starting, a community garden; if so, whom might you contact to learn more about that type of project?

———

SESSION FOUR: RESPECT, REVERENCE, AND WISDOM

CHECK-IN: How did your action step(s) from last time go? What small successes and/or obstacles are you finding as you try to implement your action step? What, if anything, would you like to do more of going forward? Do you have additional support—such as family, friends, or colleagues—who might offer assistance as you undertake your action steps? How might you tap into additional resources in your area?

The author encourages us to recognize the land, air, water, food, and myriad life forms here on Mother Earth as gifts. Indigenous Peoples have a long tradition of treating our Earth home with reverence by remaining open to the wisdom from all life-flowing sources. Learning to live in harmony and balance with our Earth is a sacred journey. A life of harmony and balance is also essential for the wellness of our planet and for the survival of our species and all living beings.

Questions to Explore

1. IDENTITY. How might you identify yourself beyond your job title, family role, or education? What are your unique gifts? Does your family name follow your mother's and grandmother's lineage? If not, why not? If you don't know your family lineage, or prefer not to identify with that heritage, what feels like home or "family" in your soul? How might you introduce yourself in a sacred way that speaks to your heart? Fill in the following:

2. I am _____, my heart's passion is _____, and I serve my community through my gift(s) of

_____.

3. NAMING. How do you refer to Earth? Does it make a difference if we identify Earth as Grandmother Earth, Gaia, Pachamama, Cosmic Mother, Mother Earth, or planet Earth? How were you taught the names of places, plants, and animals?

4. WISDOM. Do you view plants and animals as sources of wisdom? Do you view all living creatures as part of our Earth family? Do you feel connected to our global Earth family inhabitants?

5. LAND ANCESTRY. Do you know the history of the land upon which you live? Do you know the land(s) of your ancestry? What about the ancestry of the people who were on the land before you? Do you know the names given by Indigenous Peoples to the lands, plants, and animals of your area?

6. INDIGENOUS PEOPLES. If you are non-Indigenous, are you aware of the Indigenous Peoples currently living in your community and in your country? What about globally? If you are Indigenous to your homeland, are you able to share your story and your Earth knowledge with the non-Indigenous community? How might we bridge Western science with Indigenous wisdom?

7. TRUTH TELLING. What truth telling needs to happen in your community for healing? Are you aware of the atrocities enacted against Indigenous Peoples? Does your organization, school, business, or government have an Indigenous Peoples Land Acknowledgment statement? Are leadership positions in your government and local organizations held by Indigenous Peoples?

8. EXPANDING OUR COMMUNITIES. Is there an Indigenous cultural/educational center in your area? Have you visited an Indigenous cultural center or attended educational programs run by Indigenous Peoples? Are Indigenous Peoples actively involved in the scientific and educational projects in the universities and businesses in your community?

ACTION STEPS: What actions could you take to show reverence and respect for our Earth home? For example, maybe picking up litter, planting native plants for birds, or spending more time in nature. What sacred sources of wisdom benefit you personally? Do you have access to nature so you can connect with trees, birds, wind, and water? If not, do you have access to music that has soothing nature sounds? Try to do one thing before the next Earth Sustainability Circle gathering that deeply connects you to nature. What might that look like?

––––––

SESSION FIVE: FOSSIL FUEL AIR POLLUTION AND CLIMATE CHANGE

CHECK-IN: What action step(s) did you take after the last gathering and how did it go? Share if you gained anything new from that experience. Is it getting any easier to take small steps? If you haven't had time for action steps, just know that showing up for these gatherings, or giving your support to others as they share their struggles or progress, is a valuable contribution.

We need clean air to breathe. We also must recognize that the largest contributor to human-caused climate change is the burning of fossil fuels: coal, oil, and gas. To address these environmental problems, the author encourages us to look at our sources of energy for transportation, industry processes, housing, and so on. Additionally, the author points out that how we invest our money, what businesses we support, what legislative polices we enact, and what products we refuse to promote through advertisements can all serve as a means for making positive changes.

Questions to Explore

1. CLIMATE DISRUPTIONS. Has your area experienced any effects of climate change? What about neighboring areas or regions in your country? Has there been an increase in wildfires, droughts, flooding, heat waves, or storm intensity? What have been the worst climate catastrophes so far? What environmental disruptions are most affecting your local area, state, or country?

2. AIR QUALITY. Do you know if your town, city, state, or country generally has healthy air quality or poor air quality? Do you check the air quality measurements for your local area through a weather app or online website, such as Airnow.gov, that tracks Air Quality Index numbers? If you live in the United States, what is the American Lung Association report card rating for your area? What are the primary sources of air pollution in your community? What is your city, state, province, region, and country doing to mitigate climate change and reduce sources of air pollution?

3. AIR POLLUTION HEALTH CONSEQUENCES. Do you know children who suffer from asthma? What about adults with lung cancer or chronic obstructive pulmonary disease who are nonsmokers? Have you noticed your eyes becoming irritated or your throat getting scratchy during poor air quality days? Is your area subject to occasional, or frequent, hazy skies from air pollution?

4. DIVESTING FROM FOSSIL FUELS. Has your workplace, university, or city divested from fossil fuel investments? What cities, organizations, or individuals have successfully done so? If you have a retirement account, have you explored socially responsible investing? Do your credit card and banking institutions do anything to fight climate change?

5. ADVERTISEMENTS. Do the restrictions on tobacco ads help address the health challenges posed from cigarette smoking? What do you think about limiting or banning fossil fuel advertisements? Are there similarities between these industries? What challenges might come up in attempting to restrict or ban fossil fuel ads? How might limits on fossil fuel advertising be imposed?

6. CURBING AIR POLLUTION. Do you have access to walking and bicycle paths? Do you have access to affordable public transportation that operates on clean

energy? Do you know the names of your local and region-
ally elected officials? Have you ever written to your representatives to voice your concerns about climate change
and/or air pollution from the burning of fossil fuels?

7. JOINING FORCES. Which nonprofit environmental
organizations or advocacy groups in your community are
working on climate change and air quality pollution
issues? Are there any local chapters in your area?

ACTION STEPS: What are three action steps you can
take before the next Earth Sustainability Circle meeting?
If you are researching topics to learn more, that counts as
an action step. Contacting people in leadership positions
—such as individuals in charge of transportation, investments, government policies, or environmental nonprofits
—to learn more or to voice your concerns also count as
action steps. Looking into the Air Quality Index numbers
for your area is also a useful action step.

ADDITIONAL POSSIBLE ACTION STEP: Research
how your credit card, banking institution, and/or financial
investments—such as Environmental, Social, and Gover-
nance (ESG) investing or Socially Responsible Investing
(SRI)—can be used to further your Earth care values. As
You Sow, a nonprofit organization that promotes environmental and social corporate responsibility, has reports on
companies that are leading the way on sustainability.
Organizations such as Bank for Good list institutions with
a fossil free commitment.

———

SESSION SIX: EARTH-FRIENDLY INNOVATIONS

CHECK-IN: What action step(s) did you take after the last Earth Sustainability Circle gathering? Share if you learned anything from that experience. How are you handling any obstacles you have faced so far during this process? What helps you stay motivated during setbacks?

We know environmental problems have disproportionately affected poor and marginalized communities, especially predominantly Black and ethnic minority neighborhoods. On a positive note, people within their local communities are finding opportunities to adopt cleaner, Earth-friendly solutions to address the effects of climate change and to reduce pollution, including Black communities that have suffered from racist environmental policies. Solar power and green roofs are two examples of eco-friendly solutions mentioned by the author.

Questions to Explore

1. ADDRESSING THE NEEDS OF MARGINALIZED COMMUNITIES. What unique environmental pollutants and climate change disruptions are BIPOC (Black, Indigenous, People of Color) and other marginalized or impoverished communities facing? Are these environmental concerns being addressed? What do the residents of poor and marginalized communities want for their neighborhoods? What local organizations are engaged in BIPOC community care and community activism? What preventative actions and government policies are eliminating climate change risks and pollution hazards in poor and marginalized communities in your region?

2. CARBON FOOTPRINT. Do you know how to calculate the carbon footprint for your business, school, residence, or place of worship? The U.S. Environmental Protection Agency has resources for small businesses to calculate their greenhouse gas emissions and also has a household carbon footprint calculator. An easy-to-read article for businesses can be found on the Green Business Bureau website, "How to Calculate Your Carbon Footprint." Numerous websites offer this type of service.

3. REDUCING ENERGY CONSUMPTION. Have you done a utility audit of your residence, business, school, or place of worship to find ways to reduce energy consumption? For example, does your residence, business, school, or place of worship use energy-efficient lightbulbs, energy-efficient appliances, eco-friendly paper products, and have adequate insulation?

4. CLEAN ENERGY. Do the buildings in your community—such as apartments, homes, businesses, places of worship, government buildings, and schools—utilize sources of clean energy, such as solar panels, wind, or geothermal? Does the public transportation in your area operate using clean energy?

5. BUILDING SUSTAINABILITY PLANS. Are the building developers in your area installing solar panels and/or green roofs and incorporating energy-efficient, sustainability designs into their building plans? How might you support businesses that are doing so?

6. GOVERNMENT GREEN POLICIES. Are your local governmental leaders taking actions to mitigate climate change or are they burying their heads in the sand? Do your government leaders enact policies and promote incentives for making clean energy transitions, such as cost-saving measures for solar panel installation and for purchasing electric vehicles? Are there adequate penalties in place for industries that are contributing to pollution and/or climate change? How might you advocate for climate-friendly changes in your community?

ACTION STEPS: What action step are you inspired to take before the next session? This action step could be something from prior sessions that you haven't had a chance to do yet. Which businesses, nonprofit organizations, or government leaders in your community are promoting the use of alternative clean energy? Are there businesses and/or government leaders you want to support because of their Earth stewardship measures? Are there businesses or government leaders you want to stop supporting because of their harmful treatment of our Earth home or their disregard for necessary clean-energy changes?

SESSION SEVEN: PROTECTING FORESTS

CHECK-IN: What action step(s) did you take after the prior session? How are you feeling about your progress so far? Are you still finding ways to practice self-care? Do you have practices that help boost your spirits when you're feeling discouraged, such as reading a favorite quote or spending restorative time in nature?

The author states that trees are not only beautiful, they are also necessary for our survival. Saving trees, both in our urban landscapes and in old-growth forests, is critical work. Trees help temper climate change, help prevent soil erosion and flooding, provide cooling in summer, improve air quality, and create habitat for many creatures. Planting trees and preventing deforestation greatly benefits Mother Earth and all living beings. Check out the National Wildlife Federation's Trees for Wildlife program to learn more about the amazing ways in which trees provide for our Earth home.

Questions to Explore

1. PROTECTING FORESTS. Do you have forests in your region? If so, are government leaders, businesses, and nonprofit organizations in your community working to safeguard these forests? Has your community experienced flooding or heat waves due to a lack of wooded areas?

2. SUSTAINABILITY REQUIREMENTS. Does your community require the preservation of mature trees/wooded areas, wetlands, and prairies in housing and business development plans? Are community developers, zoning commissioners, and elected officials educated about sustainability practices, such as the risks of increased flooding when urban forests and old-growth forests are decimated?

3. TREE PLANTING. Do you plant trees or coordinate tree planting events at your neighborhood schools, workplace, place of worship, or other locations within your community? What about marginalized neighborhoods and dilapidated, impoverished areas? What is being done to enhance these neighborhoods with green spaces, wooded areas, and orchards?

4. PALM OIL USE. What products do you buy that contain palm oil or a palm oil derivative? Have you done an inventory of your common household items to see if they are Earth-friendly? Are there ways in which consumers can influence the goods available for us to purchase?

5. LIVING IN BALANCE AND HARMONY. Do you notice when you are out of balance physically, emotionally, mentally, or spiritually? How do you regain equilibrium in your life? Are humans living in harmony with Earth and all of her beautiful creatures? What practices might help us connect more with Mother Earth's rhythms?

ACTION STEPS: What two actions can you take to help save forests or to plant more trees in your community and/or across the globe? Do you know of nonprofit organizations working to save urban forests or rainforests that you can support with your time or resources? Are there government representatives or business leaders you can contact to voice your concerns about the health of our environment or to show your support for their efforts to improve the health and quality of our environments?

224 DIANA J. ENSIGN, J.D.

SESSION EIGHT: LISTENING TO YOUNG PEOPLE

CHECK-IN: What action step(s) did you take after the prior Earth Sustainability Circle? What challenges are you encountering? What successes have you had so far? Note, success looks different to each of us. Don't underestimate the ordinary interactions you have with others—such as a conversation with friends, family, or colleagues. Perhaps you have made small changes in your daily life? Have you given yourself time to celebrate your accomplishments?

The author spends time listening to high school students who are concerned about our environmental crisis. Members of the younger generation have insights into our culture from their unique perspective. Our youth can help everyone learn, and evolve, in new ways. It's important that we listen to the input of young people when discussing ideas about how to take better care of our planet.

Questions to Explore

1. SUPPORTING YOUTH-LED CLIMATE ACTIVISM. Are there ways by which you can show your support for youth-led environmental actions in your neighborhood, schools, organizations, and places of worship? Are the schools, businesses, and government leaders in your community supporting youth-led climate action?

2. CLOTHING CHOICES. What do you do with your old clothing? In what ways can you reduce your clothing consumption or the clothing consumption of others in your household? How might you shop more sustainably?

3. GOVERNMENTAL ACCOUNTABILITY. Are your government leaders listening to youth environmental activists and implementing policies to protect our planet for future generations?

4. MANUFACTURING HOPE. What helps you create hope when working on challenging environmental issues? How do you remain optimistic in the face of setbacks?

5. ENGAGING YOUNG PEOPLE. If you are a parent, are you listening to the ideas of your children regarding how we can take better care for our Earth home? If you are not a parent, are there ways in which you can interact with the youth in your community? Are young people in your community invited to participate in meaningful environmental discussions?

6. YOUTH EMPOWERMENT. If you are a young adult, are you engaging older adults—such as parents, grandparents, teachers, and civic leaders—in your efforts to help save the planet? How might you gain wider community support for your activism? Have you reached out to school clubs, places of worship, neighborhoods, athletic associations, government leaders, or retirement communities?

ACTION STEPS: Take one action related to the sustainable clothing discussion and/or toward engagement with young people—or an organization focused on youth. Try having a conversation with someone from a different generation to listen to their concerns about our planet. Are there ways in which you can engage the younger generation and/or their parents in a conversation about climate change and Earth care? What about contacting elected officials to let them know that you support youth-led environmental actions that aim to safeguard our Earth home?

If you are a young adult already engaged in Earth-care activism, thank you! Let your parents, teachers, and community leaders know why these issues matter and how they can better support you!

———

SESSION NINE: CREATING BETTER MODELS

CHECK-IN: What action step(s) did you take after the prior Earth Sustainability Circle session? Share what you gained from that experience. Are you finding ways to connect with your community, perhaps even venturing outside of your comfort zone? Have you connected with any local environmental nonprofit organizations?

The author notes that our homes, workplaces, schools, businesses, governments, and places of worship can all serve as healthy models for making Earth-friendly choices. Mindfulness in our daily actions —in our personal lives and in our various roles out in the world— can have a tremendous effect on the wellness of our Earth home. What we say, what we purchase, what we eat, what we choose to nurture and to protect, and how we live will ripple out into our families, our communities, and the world. As Buddhist monk Thich Nhat Hanh said, "Our life is our message." What legacy will we leave?

Questions to Explore

1. EARTH SUSTAINABILITY MODELS. Does your organization, or the places you frequent, have Earth sustainability practices? What specific environmental actions has your workplace, school, place of worship, home, or local community taken toward becoming more eco-friendly? What efforts are being made by local businesses to reduce pollution, protect nature, and address the climate crisis? Are there organizational models that you admire for "walking the talk" regarding the care of our Earth home?

2. ART. What do you think is the role of art, and the job of artists, in your community—and in the world? How might creative expression be a useful tool to address or solve some of our environmental challenges? Why does art matter, especially in environmental activism?

3. ELIMINATING SINGLE-USE PLASTICS. How much single-use plastic does your household use on a daily or weekly basis? Are there ways to reduce single-use plastic consumption in your household? How much daily or weekly plastic is being used once—and then thrown out— by your workplace or school? What about the use of plastics by businesses, governments, places of worship, and nonprofits in your area? Are they working to eliminate single-use plastics? Are there additional ways to reduce single-use plastics in your local community? Are there ways to reduce single-use plastics in your state/region or country?

4. PERSONAL VALUES. How do our values shape how we care for Mother Earth—or demonstrate our lack of Earth care? How would you answer the author's question: "What do we need to do differently to instill love for our Mother Earth?"

5. A CIRCULAR ECONOMY. Do you know of examples in your community where people are engaged in circular economy practices? How does a circular economy make a difference in consumption, waste, and pollution? Are there organizations you can contact to learn more about adopting circular economy principles in your community?

6. B-CORPORATIONS. Do you support businesses that have B-Corp certification? How might we encourage businesses to transition toward Earth-friendly and people-friendly actions? Are there additional solutions to our environmental problems not discussed by the author?

7. SUSTAINABILITY ACTION PLANS. When assessing the sustainability practices and policies of an organization—such as a school, business, government office, or nonprofit group—look into the following points:

- Does the organization have an Earth Sustainability Action Plan? Is there a director of sustainability, or an environmental consultant, whose job is to assist with sustainability initiatives?
- Does the organization recycle and prohibit single-use plastics?
- Does it have native plants, rather than invasive plants and non-native grass landscaping?
- Does it use alternative clean energy, such as solar, wind, or geothermal?
- Does it actively promote community efforts to mitigate our climate crisis through grants, resources, creation of public green spaces, environmental justice programs, and clean energy advocacy?
- Does the organization measure its carbon footprint, and is it transparent with the results?
- Has the organization divested from fossil fuel companies? Does it limit or prohibit fossil fuel advertising?
- Is the organization transparent about sustainability measures in its supply chain?
- Do the actions by the organization preserve and protect nature?
- Is the organization harming the environment —air, water, land, plants, wildlife, humans— through its actions and policies, or through a lack of eco-friendly actions and policies?

- Does it acknowledge environmental practices that need improvement and have a plan for addressing problem areas?

8. LEAVING A LEGACY. What legacy do you want to leave for future generations? Are there ways we can make a positive difference in our families and in our communities? A positive difference could be something that seems small to you but helps our Earth in some way.

ACTION STEP: Make a brief list of the organizations that you interact with on a regular basis. Find out if they have a Sustainability Statement or Sustainability Action Plan. Contact one or more of these places via letter, email, website contact form, telephone call, or in-person meeting to let them know that their sustainability practices, or lack thereof, matter to you. Is there another action step you feel inspired to take? Perhaps there are Earth-based art projects you'd like to support or artists you admire who are speaking up about saving our planet?

The next session is the last for this book's Earth Sustainability Circle gatherings. Plan a celebration for your final gathering. Consider a pitch-in with vegan or vegetarian food and healthy snacks.

———

SESSION TEN: MOVING HUMANITY FORWARD

CHECK-IN: What action step(s) did you take after the last Earth Sustainability Circle? What have you found most helpful over the course of the Earth Sustainability Circle gatherings? What ideas will you take from this group going forward? What new era in humanity will you help to create?

The author states that when we gather together with a shared vision toward a common goal, we can change the world. Sometimes we see these changes right away. Other times, we do not see the immediate results of our work. Sometimes, we do not see the results in our lifetime. Nevertheless, we know that future generations depend on the choices we make today.

Questions to Explore

1. SHIFTING OUT OF HELPLESSNESS. Do you feel less overwhelmed than when you began this journey? If so, what has most helped you shift from feeling overwhelmed to feeling empowered?

2. LIFELONG LEARNING. Are there any environmental topics that you feel especially passionate about or topics you want to dive into deeper in order to learn more?

3. EARTH STEWARDSHIP. Are there Earth-friendly practices that you plan to implement going forward, either personally or professionally? Or perhaps you learned something new from these gatherings that you found particularly helpful?

4. CONNECTING WITH NATURE. Do you have a favorite place in nature where you feel peaceful and rejuvenated? What do you most appreciate and love about our Earth home?

5. SHARING OUR GIFTS. How might your unique gifts be put to use for fostering greater awareness of the need to care for our Earth home? Perhaps you are good at event planning, organizing, artistic pursuits, advocating, letter writing, leading worship, educating, and so on. Are there ways in which you might reach out to others who are doing Earth care work?

6. COMMUNITY CARE. Are there ways to connect with people in your community—including poor and marginalized communities—to assist in implementing healthy Earth care practices? What about ways to work together to ensure that legislative environmental policies benefit the health of all our communities rather than serving only economic interests?

7. CELEBRATE SMALL SUCCESSES. What is your biggest takeaway from the Earth Sustainability Circles? Are there organizations, friends, or businesses that would benefit from participating in Earth Sustainability Circles?

ACTION STEP: Celebrate your Earth Sustainability Circle efforts and accomplishments! What are you grateful for today? How will you stay connected with each other?

———

Spread the Word: Collectively, we are working toward healthy people, healthy communities, and a healthy planet. We will usher in a new world, together.

Gratitude and thanks for your loving contributions to Mother Earth!

ACKNOWLEDGMENTS

Profound thanks to my husband, Dave, whose extensive conservation knowledge as retired state biologist for the Natural Resources Conservation Service and passion for habitat restoration and invasive species eradication greatly aided the writing of this book. Gratitude to my daughters, Emmeline and Indigo, who always inspire my creative dreams. They are the reason I do this work.

This book rests on the knowledge of numerous scientists, friends, teachers, writers, activists, community leaders, and organizations. I am extremely grateful to the people who took time to meet with me during this project, as well as the people I have not personally met but whose work in caring for our Earth home motivates me to learn and do more. While I cannot list every person and organization that influenced this book in some way, I would like to thank the following individuals for speaking with me and/or assisting with the book content:

Pat Bittner, farmer, focused on regenerative farming, and Gabe Brown, author of *Dirt to Soil*; Wayne Valliere (Lac du Flambeau Band of Lake Superior Ojibwe), language and cultural educator and Ojibwe birch-bark canoe maker; Nils "Buster" Landin (Anishinaabe/Tlingit), graduate assistant at Purdue University Native American Educational and Cultural Center; Billie Warren, a member of the Pokagon Band of Potawatomi; Carole Bishop and Bryan L. Morrison of Pure Eating Way (a minority and woman owned plant-based whole food company); Ellen Jacquart, ecologist, Indiana Native Plant Society and Monroe County Identify and Remove Invasive Species (MC-IRIS), formerly with The Nature Conservancy; Dr. Candace Corson, MD, CEO of Corson Wellness; James Mosley, NAACP – Evansville, chair environmental justice; Paula Brooks, environmental justice director for the Hoosier Environmental Council; Kate Hammel, Sycamore Land Trust; Leslie Webb, co-founder and president, Carmel Green Initiative; Amanda Shepherd, regional director of the Sierra Club; Zach Schalk, Solar United Neighbors; Reverend Amber Good, Teter Organic Farm; Ray Wilson, engineer and solar advocate; Carl Gibson, Ivy Tech Physics teacher; Rae Schnapp, PhD, conservation director of Indiana Forest Alliance; Breubeuf Jesuit Preparatory School students Madison Bacani, Claire Curran, and Ben Hutchinson, and their teacher, Nick Klinger, director for community service/department chair; and Barbara Simpson, vice president, Friends of Goose Pond.

Additionally, I gained valuable information from creation care initiatives at Saint Mary-of-the-Woods, St. Thomas Aquinas, Unitarian Universalist Church of Indianapolis, St. Luke's United Methodist Church, and Second Presbyterian Church (farmers' market), and from events at the Native American Educational and Cultural Center at Purdue University, Indiana Forest Alliance (Wild & Scenic Film Festival), University of Indianapolis and Indiana Humanities (panel of speakers at the Environmental Justice in the Circle City, Richard M. Fairbanks Symposium), and Indiana University Environmental Resilience Institute (panel of speakers at the Indiana Sustainability and Resilience Conference).

Thanks to T. Payne at Arcane Book Cover Designs for an excellent cover design and to Tom Casalini for my

Author photo. As always, I am extremely grateful for the professional expertise of Lè Weaver at CircleWebWorks—not only for a superb website design but also for their unflinching encouragement of my writing projects. I am incredibly fortunate to have friends, too many to name, who lift me up when I feel discouraged. Thank you!

Finally, I would like to acknowledge the support for this project from the Indiana Arts Commission Creative Entrepreneur On-Ramp grant. The arts help sustain and guide us during our most challenging times.

INDIANA ARTS
COMMISSION

ADDITIONAL RESOURCES

The following books were used as resources during this writing project:

A Sand County Almanac, Aldo Leopold, 1966, A Ballantine Book.
Blue Covenant: The Global Water Crisis and the Coming Battle for the Right to Water, Maude Barlow, 2007, The New Press.
Dirt to Soil: One Family's Journey into Regenerative Agriculture: Gabe Brown, 2018, Chelsea Green Publishing.
Greta Thunberg: No One is Too Small to Make a Difference, 2018, Penguin Books.
Saving Us: A Climate Scientist's Case for Hope and Healing in a Divided World, Katharine Hayhoe, 2021, Simon & Shuster.
Silent Spring, Rachel Carson, 1962, First Mariner Books.

I also relied on information contained in numerous articles, organization websites, and environmental news sources. These sources, to the best of my ability, are listed throughout the book. I am a spiritual writer, not a scientist or academic researcher. As such, this book is intended to be of a general nature only. Please consult directly the scientists and academic experts for up-to-date information, scientific data, and verification of independent research.

ABOUT THE AUTHOR

Diana J. Ensign, JD, is an award-winning author and essayist who writes about the human spirit. For over two decades, she has explored spiritual teachings and wisdom traditions from a variety of sources. Two of Ensign's books are Independent Publisher Book Awards (IPPY) Gold Medal Winners. The IPPY Awards showcase the best books from throughout North America and recognize merit and reward authors who take chances and break new ground. Ensign is also a two-time Individual Advancement Program grant recipient and a Creative Entrepreneur On-Ramp grant recipient awarded by the Indiana Arts Commission. In addition, she received a Beacon Fund grant for an outdoor labyrinth project.

Born in Florida and raised in Michigan, Ensign graduated from the University of Michigan in Ann Arbor and Wayne State University Law School in Detroit. She is married with two adult children. Ensign currently resides in Indiana where she supports a lengthy list of nonprofit organizations. She cares deeply about the environment, children, healing, and amplifying the voices of marginalized groups. Spirituality and compassionate action are the cornerstones of her life.

Ensign also writes the popular "Spirituality for Daily Living" blog found on her website. A frequent speaker and workshop facilitator, she can be contacted via her website: www.dianaensign.com

PREVIOUS BOOKS BY DIANA J. ENSIGN

A Moment of Calm*: Meditative and Reflective Readings for Inner Peace* (SpiritHawk Life Publications, 2020).

Whatever our current situation, we can all benefit from more peace and calm in our lives. With these beautifully composed meditative essays, Diana J. Ensign offers the reader an opportunity to delve deep and discover the inner peace, healing, and joy available to us in ordinary moments.

"Brilliant yet simple! A beautiful pathway to a deeper integration of personal awareness and to a miraculous, nourishing life." —Christine Lily Kessler, artist, author, energy healer

The Freedom to Be*: Stories from Transgender Youth, Adults, and Their Families* (SpiritHawk Life Publications, 2020). Outstanding Book of the Year, IPPY Gold Medal Winner!

With compassionate listening, Diana J. Ensign offers insightful narratives explaining how parents, teachers, healthcare providers, neighbors, and friends can create supportive communities for transgender individuals. A percentage of the profits go to support LGBTQ organizations. This social justice project was made possible by an IAP grant from the Indiana Arts Commission.

"As a parent to a transgender child, I recommend The Freedom to Be *to family members, friends, and community members who want ideas on how to best support transgender individuals."*

—*Steph B., parent*

Heart Guide: *True Stories of Grief and Healing* (SpiritHawk Life Publications, 2017), IPPY Gold Medal Winner!

In this book, Diana J. Ensign shares intimate and poignant guidance for people who are grieving the death of a loved one. These intimate, personal stories highlight the myriad and unexpected ways people cope with traumatic loss.

"Frank, warm, unflinching, and compassionate—a heartfelt work that explores sorrow and healing." —Kirkus Reviews

Traveling Spirit: *Daily Tools for Your Life's Journey* (Balboa Press, 2013).

This is the perfect book for anyone seeking help and guidance with human suffering. Here, Diana J. Ensign provides spiritual practices for dealing with life's challenges. A percentage of the profits from *Traveling Spirit* go to support the Lambi Fund of Haiti (working on reforestation in Haiti, along with women's and girl's health, nutrition, and education).

"Traveling Spirit is an honest, practical, and transformational blueprint for living a joyously spirited life." —Virginia R. Mollenkott, PhD, author

———

Signed copies of Diana J. Ensign's books are available on her website: **www.dianaensign.com.** Purchasing directly from the author supports her work. Book copies are also available at Amazon, Ingram, and Barnes & Noble, and they are available to order through independent bookstores. If you enjoy her books, please leave a review. You can also request that your local library carry copies of Diana's books.

www.ingramcontent.com/pod-product-compliance
Lightning Source LLC
Chambersburg PA
CBHW031120020426

42333CB00012B/168